Investing Workbook Series: Stocks ❶ ❷ ❸

How to Refine Your Stock

Published by John Wiley & Sons, Inc., Hoboken, New Jersey.
Published simultaneously in Canada.

For general information about our other products and services, please contact our Customer Care Department within the United States at 800-762-2974, outside the United States at 317-572-3993 or fax 317-572-4002.

Wiley also publishes its books in a variety of electronic formats. Some content that appears in print may not be available in electronic books. For more information about Wiley products, visit our Web site at www.wiley.com.

ISBN: 0-471-71961-7

Printed in the United States of America
10 9 8 7 6 5 4 3 2 1

Introduction

There is no doubt that investing in stocks is a worthwhile endeavor. Over the long term, no other investment type has performed better.

Unfortunately, investing in stocks is not easy. Numerous things need to be learned before you can understand what buying a stock really means. Anyone can pull up quotes and blindly trade, but it takes much more effort to become a true investor. We aim to make this effort as painless as possible.

The goal of this workbook series is to set you on the path to becoming an informed, educated stock investor. We can't promise you will make millions in the stock market next year after purchasing and going through these workbooks, but we can say with certainty you will gain knowledge that will provide you with a solid base from which to start your stock-investing career. You and your family's finances should be better off as a result.

Though the three books in this series are designed to be used with one another, they can be used individually and are of increasing difficulty.

Workbook #1, *How to Get Started in Stocks*, is intended for readers who are totally new to investing. It will help those with little to no stock-investing experience quickly get up to speed on the main concepts. The book explains why you should consider investing in stocks in the first place, what a stock actually is, and the basics of how a company works, and it also answers many of the other common questions new investors might have.

Workbook #2, *How to Select Winning Stocks*, is much more focused. It details how to read a company's financial statements, how to locate quality companies for potential investment, and how to actually go about placing a value on a business. New investors should certainly go through Workbook #1 first, while those who have bought stocks before will probably be fine skipping straight to this book.

Workbook #3, *How to Refine Your Stock Strategy*, is the most advanced of the series. Even experienced investors proficient in analyzing companies may find this an enlightening read into how we think about stocks at Morningstar. In this book, we touch on the investment styles of some of the great investors of our time, share some of the insights and strategies we here at Morningstar have come up with, and finally offer pointers on building and maintaining a stock portfolio.

Each workbook lesson is divided into four distinct sections as outlined below. As you will see, going through these workbooks is intended to be an interactive experience.

Lessons: The main text of each lesson is designed to give you an overview of a particular topic, along with plenty of real-life examples and tips for putting your newly gained knowledge into action while investing.

Investor's Checklist: These scannable lists provide you with the most important take-home messages from the lessons. Use the Investor's Checklists to brush up on what you've just learned and as a quick reference of the most salient points to remember.

Quizzes: The quizzes help ensure that you've indeed mastered the key concepts in the lesson. Answers to each of the quiz questions are at the back of each book.

Worksheets: The worksheets are designed to help you put the key concepts of each lesson into practice. A worksheet answer key is also at the back of each book. Though there is sometimes no right or wrong answer to these exercises, the answer key will in these cases reinforce the points being made.

In addition, each workbook has the following at the back:

Additional Morningstar Resources: Morningstar's Investing Series is designed as an introduction to Morningstar's approach. We have numerous other products for stock investors of all experience levels.

Recommended Readings: This is a list of some of Morningstar's favorite books about stock investing.

Investing Terms: Though each lesson assumes no previous experience in investing (beyond reading the previous lessons in the series), the Investing Terms section gives more in-depth definitions of the main terms used in the text.

While this investing series will be of the most value to those who have the most to learn, even the most seasoned investors will find parts of it enlightening. After all, one can never learn too much when engaged in an intellectual exercise.

Good luck on your journey, and may happy returns follow your effort!

Acknowledgments

Developing this workbook series was a collaborative effort with scores of Morningstar people deserving credit. There may be only one name on the back cover, yet all the following stock analysts deserve special thanks for contributing significant portions of the content contained within:

Ryan Batchelor
Joel Bloomer
Eric Chenoweth
Michael Cumming
Sumit Desai
Lauren DeSanto
Mark Hugh Sam
Curt Morrison
Josh Peters
Toan Tran
Jerome Van Der Ghinst

Product manager Alla Spivak shepherded all the books in this series from start to finish, making sure we hit our deadlines. With three books in the pipeline at once, her juggling was impressive.

Superstar copy editor Jason Stipp worked very hard to make sure the prose was clear and the grammar correct. Many of his weekends were spent making this a better product. Morningstar's design staff, notably Lisa Lindsay, David Silva, and David Williams, developed the books' design, melding ideas and words into a pleasing format.

Director of operations Mike Porter, former director of securities analysis Amy Arnott, and chief of securities analysis Haywood Kelly provided time from their busy schedules to give valuable feedback in the editing process.

They made sure all the bases were being hit and that the messages were consistent with the Morningstar framework. David Pugh, our editor at John Wiley & Sons, also provided valuable guidance.

Morningstar's director of stock analysis, Pat Dorsey, deserves thanks for creating and molding the investment philosophy and concepts we have distilled here. I also owe a large debt to Pat as well as all of the stock analysts on Morningstar's natural resources team for affording me time away from my "day job" to create this series.

Catherine Odelbo has earned a tip of the cap for developing the series' concept. As leading architect and head of Morningstar's Individual Investor business unit, she has always carried the torch for Morningstar's "Investors First" motto. Of course, I'm incredibly grateful to Morningstar founder Joe Mansueto. This is all possible due to Catherine and Joe's vision, leadership, and true belief in the value of independent equity research.

Finally, the books in this series could not have been written without sacrifice and understanding from my family. To them, I owe a special debt.

—*Paul Larson*

Contents

Insights from Morningstar

Lesson 301: The Fat-Pitch Strategy   3

Lesson 302: Psychology and Investing   13

Lesson 303: The Case for Dividends   27

Lesson 304: 20 Stock-Investing Tips   43

Strategies of the Greats

Lesson 305: Deep Value—Benjamin Graham   57

Lesson 306: Holding Superior Growth—Philip Fisher   71

Lesson 307: Great Companies at Reasonable Prices—Warren Buffett   87

Lesson 308: Know What You Own—Peter Lynch   99

Lesson 309: The Rest of the Hall of Fame   113

Rounding Out Your Portfolio

Lesson 310: Constructing a Portfolio   129

Lesson 311: Introduction to Options   141

Lesson 312: Unconventional Equities   153

Additional Morningstar Resources   169

Recommended Readings   171

Quiz Answer Key   175

Worksheet Answer Key   183

Investing Terms   195

Formulas Reference   225

Insights from Morningstar

Lesson 301: The Fat-Pitch Strategy

"All I can tell them is pick a good one and sock it."—*Babe Ruth*

In baseball, a batter who watches three pitches go past just inside the strike zone will be called out by the umpire. Also, as many baseball fans know, the strike zone from one umpire to the next can be a different size. Baseball players thus often have an incentive to swing at pitches they would rather not, out of fear of being called out.

Many investors, especially professional money managers, think about investing like it's a baseball game. Because they aim to beat the indexes they are being scored against, professional money managers feel a lot of pressure to get base hits, doubles, triples, and home runs in order to earn their keep. Out of fear of being "called out," they might swing at pitches that may be just inside the strike zone, even though they may prefer to watch those pitches go by. In other words, investors often forget their valuation discipline and think about investing like it's a baseball game—three called strikes and you're out. So they swing away.

But what if the rules of baseball were different? What if a batter could watch any number of pitches go by, waiting for the perfect "fat pitch" to come along before swinging? Baseball will never adopt this rule, of course—games would last too long and pitchers would bemoan their escalating ERAs. But as an investor, you can (and should) play by these rules.

You can significantly raise your investment batting average by waiting for the pitcher—Mr. Market—to throw you a nice fat pitch right down the middle of the strike zone. Unless the market throws a pitch that you're very confident in swinging at, you can stand by and watch strike after strike be thrown without worrying about being called out, because, unlike in baseball, there is no penalty for being patient in investing. With the market pitching, you can let as many curveballs, knuckleballs, and sliders go by as you like until you see the one you want to hit.

The fat-pitch strategy that we have developed here at Morningstar has five parts:

1. Look for Wide-Moat Companies.

As we've described in the previous workbooks, companies with wide economic moats reside in profitable industries and have long-term structural advantages versus competitors. These companies are fat pitches with predictable earnings, returns on capital higher than the cost of capital, and long-term staying power.

The beauty of a wide-moat company is that the odds are pretty high that the actual intrinsic value of the firm will increase over time, leading to higher shareholder value. In other words, time is on your side with these companies. By contrast, companies with no economic moat generally destroy shareholder value over time—when you buy a no-moat company, you're making a speculative bet that the stock will bounce up just long enough for you to sell it. That's a very tough game to play, and generally only seasoned pros should attempt it.

Keeping a Wide-Moat Watch List	We recommend maintaining a watch list of wide-moat companies that you consistently monitor for any opportunities. You can also input and manage your watch list using Morningstar.com's Portfolio Manager. Premium subscribers can also use Morningstar.com as a resource to see which companies we think have wide moats.
	Once you've compiled a list of wide-moat stocks, you can set up alerts that will inform you when certain events occur, such as when a stock's price drops below the price at which you'd consider buying it.

2. Always Have a Margin of Safety.

Instead of buying a stock based on what everyone else is doing, buy a stock only when it's selling at a decent margin of safety to your estimate of its fair value. Don't even think about the overall direction of the stock market because that's impossible to predict with any consistency. By doing this, you'll need to exercise a lot of discipline and wrestle with the fear of missing out on a market rally. Patience is indeed a virtue when using this approach because oftentimes it may take many months, or longer, before a fat-pitch opportunity presents itself.

Although you may feel at times that the market is running away from you, and a fat pitch may never come around, rest assured that there will be opportunities in the future, and you'll be poised to swing away. Think only about individual wide-moat companies; if you find one where the price is irrationally low relative to its long-term intrinsic value, consider buying it. If not, hold off for a fatter pitch.

Obviously, to determine whether a particular stock is trading with a sufficient margin of safety, you must have some sort of an estimate of what you think the stock is worth. These workbooks have given you enough information that you should start to be able to place a value on a stock. We encourage you to practice this repeatedly to hone your valuation skills.

Also, you must determine how much of a margin of safety you'll require before buying a stock. If the firm is not very risky, you could be content with a 15%-20% discount to its fair value. If the firm is riskier than average, you may demand a 30%-40% discount. Ultimately, it's your decision.

The beauty of fat-pitch investing is that it has two built-in factors which help offset the risk that your fair value estimate is wrong. First, by requiring a margin of safety, you've given yourself some "error cushion," just in case your estimate was too high. Second, by purchasing wide-moat companies, chances are high that the firm will increase in value over time. Thus, even if your estimates were way off, the firm—and its stock price—will likely appreciate in value, eventually catching up to your fair value estimate. In effect, by buying wide-moat companies, you have another margin of safety built into your investment.

3. Don't Be Afraid to Hold Cash.

Holding cash is like holding an option—the option to take advantage of volatility in the market. The value of this option rises when market volatility rises. Thus, when the volatile stock market provides you an opportunity to buy wide-moat companies at bargain prices, you'll be ready with cash in hand to take advantage of the irrationality.

Many market participants often neglect this important aspect of investing and stay fully invested at all times. For instance, many professionals getting paid to invest other people's money feel they are actually required to stay fully invested even if there's a lack of fat-pitch opportunities. Thus, when the market drops, they often can't do anything but watch (or worse, sell out near the bottom).

Being fully invested at all times goes hand-in-hand with the professional's focus on relative returns—beating an index. For example, if the market drops by 10% in a year, but the fictional Relative Return Fund dropped only by 8%, Relative Return's manager has provided value because the fund had a better return relative to the market. However, had you invested in this fund, you'd still be 8% poorer, not exactly anything to cheer about.

We argue that individual investors should care more about absolute returns (how much money did you make) and less about relative returns (did you beat a benchmark). So if the market isn't throwing you fat pitches, just hold on to your cash and wait until it does, because fat-pitch investments are much more likely to provide strong absolute returns over time.

4. Don't Be Afraid to Hold Relatively Few Stocks.

There are very few good ideas in any given year—Warren Buffett has said he's happy to have even one. For the rest of us (i.e., those without the need to invest several billion dollars to make a difference in their portfolios), there may be five or six good ideas a year. In any event, if you feel the need to hold more than 20 stocks, you probably aren't using the fat-pitch approach—more than likely you're speculating and trying to diversify away the risks of your speculations by holding lots of different names. Remember, it takes great patience to be a fat-pitch investor, but when opportunities present themselves (nice fat pitches right down the middle), you should buy boldly (swing away).

We caution you, however, that it's risky to hold a concentrated portfolio (few positions) unless you do three things:

1. Buy only wide-moat companies, which will increase in intrinsic value over time.
2. Buy them only at a significant discount to fair value (a margin of safety).
3. Have a time horizon of at least three years on each pick you make. It may take this long (or longer) for the market to recognize the value of a company.

If you aren't willing to follow these three rules on each and every stock you buy, then you probably need more diversification in your portfolio. (We'll talk much more about portfolio construction in Lesson 310.)

5. Don't Trade Very Often.

If you're using the fat-pitch approach, you won't need to trade very often because you'll hold only wide-moat companies. By definition, a wide-moat company has long-term advantages and creates shareholder value year-in and year-out. Because a wide-moat firm creates value each year, its fair value tends to increase over time. These are the only types of stocks in which a buy-and-hold strategy works well because the odds are in your favor that the actual underlying value will continue increasing over time. As we mentioned earlier, when you buy a company with no moat, you are making a bet that it will bounce up just long enough for you to sell it.

Think of it this way: Investing is nothing more than a game of probabilities. No matter how diligent you are, your fair value estimate for a stock will never be exactly right. It's really just an estimate of what a stock is worth under the most likely scenario for future earnings growth and profitability. Thus, there's always less than a 100% probability that you'll be right about a stock pick. Given that the odds are below 100%, there's little point in trading from one stock to another frequently; your odds of being "right" on the new pick are probably only a little higher than the odds of being wrong on the current pick.

Add to this the costs of trading—including taxes, bid-ask spreads, and commissions—and the odds of generating higher returns by trading frequently are worse than simply buying great stocks at good prices and holding them for three years or more.

The Bottom Line

By following the fat-pitch approach to stock investing, we think you can tremendously improve your odds of investment success. Although it requires plenty of discipline and patience, you should be able to earn strong returns over the long term by buying only those stocks that present a nice fat-pitch opportunity.

Investor's Checklist

► The fat-pitch strategy is based on a baseball analogy. Instead of watching borderline pitches go by, batters often swing away because they fear being called out on strikes. Similarly, many investors—instead of waiting for fantastic investment opportunities (fat pitches)—choose to buy stocks that they may not be too enthusiastic about, out of fear of being left behind by the market.

► There are no called strikes in investing.

► Individual investors often have an edge over professionals because individuals are not required to be fully invested at all times. Thus, they can patiently wait for fat pitches to come along without being worried about being called out.

► The five steps of the fat-pitch approach to stock investing are:

1. Look for wide-moat companies.
2. Always have a margin of safety.
3. Don't be afraid to hold cash.
4. Don't be afraid to hold relatively few stocks.
5. Don't trade very often.

Quiz

Answers to this quiz can be found on page 175

1   Which of the following is not one of the five steps of the fat-pitch approach?

a	Have a margin of safety.
b	Maintain a very diversified portfolio.
c	Don't trade very often.

2   Is it a detriment to fat-pitch investors to hold cash when the market is rising?

a	Yes.
b	No.
c	Maybe so.

3   A wide-moat company is typically characterized as having:

a	Long-term structural advantages over its competition.
b	Returns on capital lower than its cost of capital.
c	A perpetually cheap stock price.

4   Which of the following is not a reason that investors should refrain from trading often?

a	Costs of trading—taxes, commissions, and bid-ask spreads—can add up.
b	Once a stock is purchased, it should never be sold.
c	The odds of being "right" on a new pick aren't much higher than the odds of being "right" on your current fat-pitch holdings.

5   The fat-pitch approach to stock investing is best described as?

a	Buying average companies at below-average prices.
b	Buying above-average companies at below-average prices.
c	Buying above-average companies at average prices.

Worksheet

1   In your own words, how would you characterize the fat-pitch approach to stock investing?

Answers to this worksheet can be found on page 183

2   To help you remember, list the five steps of the fat-pitch approach:

1.

2.

3.

4.

5.

3   Explain why individual investors actually have some advantages over professional money managers:

Lesson 302: Psychology and Investing

"Man prefers to believe what he prefers to be true."—*Francis Bacon*

Successful investing is hard, but it doesn't require genius. In fact, Warren Buffett once quipped, "Success in investing doesn't correlate with I.Q. once you're above the level of 25. Once you have ordinary intelligence, what you need is the temperament to control the urges that get other people into trouble in investing." As much as anything else, successful investing requires something perhaps even more rare: the ability to identify and overcome one's own psychological weaknesses.

Over the past 20 years, psychology has permeated our culture in many ways. More recently its influences have taken hold in the field of behavioral finance, spawning an array of academic papers and learned tomes that attempt to explain why people make financial decisions that are contrary to their own interests.

Experts in the field of behavioral finance have a lot to offer in terms of understanding psychology and the behaviors of investors, particularly the mistakes that they make. Much of the field attempts to extrapolate larger, macro trends of influence, such as how human behavior might move the market.

In this lesson we'd prefer to focus on how the insights from the field of behavioral finance can benefit individual investors. Primarily, we're interested in how we can learn to spot and correct investing mistakes in order to yield greater profits.

Some insights behavioral finance has to offer read like common sense, but with more syllables.

Overconfidence

Overconfidence refers to our boundless ability as human beings to think that we're smarter or more capable than we really are. It's what leads 82% of people to say that they are in the top 30% of safe drivers, for example. Moreover, when people say that they're 90% sure of something, studies show that they're right only about 70% of the time. Such optimism isn't always bad. Certainly we'd have a difficult time dealing with life's many setbacks if we were die-hard pessimists.

However, overconfidence hurts us as investors when we believe that we're better able to spot the next Microsoft than another investor is. Odds are, we're not. (Nothing personal.)

Studies show that overconfident investors trade more rapidly because they think they know more than the person on the other side of the trade. Trading rapidly costs plenty, and rarely rewards the effort. We'll repeat yet again that trading costs in the form of commissions, taxes, and losses on the bid-ask spread have been shown to be a serious damper on annualized returns. These frictional costs will always drag returns down.

One of the things that drive rapid trading, in addition to overconfidence in our abilities, is the illusion of control. Greater participation in our investments can make us feel more in control of our finances, but there is a degree to which too much involvement can be detrimental, as studies of rapid trading have demonstrated.

Selective Memory

Another danger that overconfident behavior might lead to is selective memory. Few of us want to remember a painful event or experience in the past, particularly one that was of our own doing. In terms of investments we certainly don't want to remember those stock calls that we missed (had I only bought eBay in 1998), much less those that proved to be mistakes which ended in losses.

The more confident we are, the more such memories threaten our self-image. How can we be such good investors if we made those mistakes in the past? Instead of remembering the past accurately, in fact, we will remember it selectively so that it suits our needs and preserves our self-image.

Incorporating information in this way is a form of correcting for cognitive dissonance, a well-known theory in psychology. Cognitive dissonance posits that we are uncomfortable holding two seemingly disparate ideas, opinions, beliefs, attitudes, or in this case, behaviors, at once, and our psyche will somehow need to correct for this.

Correcting for a poor investment choice of the past, particularly if we see ourselves as skilled traders now, warrants selectively adjusting our memory of that poor investment choice. "Perhaps it really wasn't such a bad decision selling that stock?" Or, "Perhaps we didn't lose as much money as we thought?" Over time, our memory of the event will likely not be accurate but will be well integrated into a whole picture of how we need to see ourselves.

Keep Score

To avoid overconfidence in investing, it's a good idea to document and review investment records on a periodic basis. It's easy to remember the one stock that gained 50% in a single day, but records may reveal that most of our investments are under water for the year. Checking every couple weeks will do, since looking at performance on a daily or hourly basis is not likely to be insightful, and may even spur you to make hasty decisions. Either way, tracking your actual performance will not only help you keep overconfidence in check, but it will also help you identify and learn from your mistakes.

Another type of selective memory is representativeness, which is a mental shortcut that causes us to give too much weight to recent evidence—such as short-term performance numbers—and too little weight to the evidence from the more distant past. As a result, we'll give too little weight to the real odds of an event happening.

Self-Handicapping

Researchers have also observed a behavior that could be considered the opposite of overconfidence. Self-handicapping bias occurs when we try to explain any possible future poor performance with a reason that may or may not be true.

An example of self-handicapping is when we say we're not feeling good prior to a presentation, so if the presentation doesn't go well, we'll have an explanation. Or it's when we confess to our ankle being sore just before running onto the field for a big game. If we don't quite play well, maybe it's because our ankle was hurting.

As investors, we may also succumb to self-handicapping, perhaps by admitting that we didn't spend as much time researching a stock as we normally had done in the past, just in case the investment doesn't turn out quite as well as expected. Both overconfidence and self-handicapping behaviors are common among investors, but they aren't the only negative tendencies that can impact our overall investing success.

Loss Aversion

It's no secret, for example, that many investors will focus obsessively on one investment that's losing money, even if the rest of their portfolio is in the black. This behavior is called loss aversion.

Investors have been shown to be more likely to sell winning stocks in an effort to "take some profits," while at the same time not wanting to accept defeat in the case of the losers. Philip Fisher wrote in his excellent book *Common Stocks and Uncommon Profits* that, "More money has probably been lost by investors holding a stock they really did not want until they could 'at least come out even' than from any other single reason."

Regret also comes into play with loss aversion. It may lead us to be unable to distinguish between a bad decision and a bad outcome. We regret a bad outcome, such as a stretch of weak performance from a given stock, even if we chose the investment for all the right reasons. In this case, regret can lead us to make a bad sell decision, such as selling a solid company at a bottom instead of buying more.

It also doesn't help that we tend to feel the pain of a loss more strongly than we do the pleasure of a gain. It's this unwillingness to accept the pain early that might cause us to "ride losers too long" in the vain hope that they'll turn around and won't make us face the consequences of our decisions.

Sunk Costs

Another factor driving loss aversion is the sunk cost fallacy. This theory states that we are unable to ignore the "sunk costs" of a decision, even when those costs are unlikely to be recovered.

One example of this would be if we purchased expensive theater tickets only to learn prior to attending the performance that the play was terrible. Since we paid for the tickets, we would be far more likely to attend the play than we would if those same tickets had been given to us by a friend. Rational behavior would suggest that regardless of whether or not we purchased the tickets, if we heard the play was terrible, we would choose to go or not go based on our interest. Instead, our inability to ignore the sunk costs of poor investments causes us to fail to evaluate a situation such as this on its own merits. Sunk costs may also prompt us to hold on to a stock even as the underlying business falters, rather than cutting our losses. Had the dropping stock been a gift, perhaps we wouldn't hang on quite so long.

Anchoring

Ask New Yorkers to estimate the population of Chicago, and they'll anchor on the number they know—the population of the Big Apple—and adjust down, but not enough. Ask people in Milwaukee to guess the number of people in Chicago and they'll anchor on the number they know and go up, but not enough. When estimating the unknown, we cleave to what we know.

Investors often fall prey to anchoring. They get anchored on their own estimates of a company's earnings, or on last year's earnings. For investors, anchoring behavior manifests itself in placing undue emphasis on recent performance since this may be what instigated the investment decision in the first place.

When an investment is lagging, we may hold on to it because we cling to the price we paid for it, or its strong performance just before its decline, in an effort to "break even" or get back to what we paid for it. We may cling to subpar companies for years, rather than dumping them and getting on with our investment life. It's costly to hold on to losers, though, and we may miss out on putting those invested funds to better use.

Overcoming Anchoring | It may be helpful to ask yourself the following questions about your stocks: Would I buy this investment again? And if not, why do I continue to own it? Truthfully answering these questions can help you sever the anchors that may be a drag on your rational decision making.

Confirmation Bias

Another risk that stems from both overconfidence and anchoring involves how we look at information. Too often we extrapolate our own beliefs without realizing it and engage in confirmation bias, or treating information that supports what we already believe, or want to believe, more favorably.

For instance, if we've had luck owning Honda cars, we will likely be more inclined to believe information that supports our own good experience owning them, rather than information to the contrary. If we've purchased a mutual fund concentrated in health-care stocks, we may overemphasize positive information about the sector and discount whatever negative news we hear about how these stocks are expected to perform.

Hindsight bias also plays off of overconfidence and anchoring behavior. This is the tendency to re-evaluate our past behavior surrounding an event or decision knowing the actual outcome. Our judgment of a previous decision becomes biased to accommodate the new information. For example, knowing the outcome of a stock's performance, we may adjust our reasoning for purchasing it in the first place. This type of "knowledge updating" can keep us from viewing past decisions as objectively as we should.

Mental Accounting

If you've ever heard friends say that they can't spend a certain pool of money because they're planning to use it for their vacation, you've witnessed mental accounting in action. Most of us separate our money into buckets—this money is for the kids' college education, this money is for our retirement, this money is for the house. Heaven forbid that we spend the house money on a vacation.

Investors derive some benefits from this behavior. Earmarking money for retirement may prevent us from spending it frivolously. Mental accounting becomes a problem, though, when we categorize our funds without looking at the bigger picture. One example of this would be how we view a tax refund. While we might diligently place any extra money left over from our regular income into savings, we often view tax refunds as "found money" to be spent more frivolously. Since tax refunds are in fact our earned income, they should not be considered this way.

For gambling aficionados this effect can be referred to as "house money." We're much more likely to take risks with house money than with our own. For example, if we go to the roulette table with $100 and win another $200, we're more likely to take a bigger risk with that $200 in winnings than we would if the money was our own to begin with. There's a perception that the money isn't really ours and wasn't earned, so it's okay to take more risks with it. This is risk we'd be unlikely to take if we'd spent time working for that $200 ourselves.

Similarly, if our taxes were correctly adjusted so that we received that refund in portions all year long as part of our regular paycheck, we might be less inclined to go out and impulsively purchase that Caribbean cruise or flat-screen television.

In investing, just remember that money is money, no matter whether the funds in a brokerage account are derived from hard-earned savings, an inheritance, or realized capital gains.

Framing Effect

One other form of mental accounting is worth noting. The framing effect addresses how a reference point, oftentimes a meaningless benchmark, can affect our decision.

Let's assume, for example, that we decide to buy that television after all. But just before paying $500 for it, we realize it's $100 cheaper at a store down the street. In this case, we are quite likely to make that trip down the street and buy the less expensive television. If, however, we're buying a new set of living room furniture and the price tag is $5,000, we are unlikely to go down the street to the store selling it for $4,900. Why? Aren't we still saving $100?

Unfortunately, we tend to view the discount in relative, rather than absolute terms. When we were buying the television, we were saving 20% by going to the second shop, but when we were buying the living room furniture, we were saving only 2%. So it looks like $100 isn't always worth $100 depending on the situation.

The best way to avoid the negative aspects of mental accounting is to concentrate on the total return of your investments, and to take care not to think of your "budget buckets" so discretely that you fail to see how some seemingly small decisions can make a big impact.

Herding

There are thousands and thousands of stocks out there. Investors cannot know them all. In fact, it's a major endeavor to really know even a few of them. But people are bombarded with stock ideas from brokers, television, magazines, Web sites, and other places. Inevitably, some decide that the latest idea they've heard is a better idea than a stock they own (preferably one that's up, at least), and they make a trade.

Unfortunately, in many cases the stock has come to the public's attention because of its strong previous performance, not because of an improvement in the underlying business. Following a stock tip, under the assumption that others have more information, is a form of herding behavior.

This is not to say that investors should necessarily hold whatever investments they currently own. Some stocks should be sold, whether because the underlying businesses have declined or their stock prices simply exceed their intrinsic value. But it is clear that many individual (and institutional) investors hurt themselves by making too many buy and sell decisions for too many fallacious reasons. We can all be much better investors when we learn to select stocks carefully and for the right reasons, and then actively block out the noise. Any temporary comfort derived from investing with the crowd or following a market guru can lead to fading performance or inappropriate investments for your particular goals.

The Bottom Line

In this brief overview of behavioral finance, we've touched on the major tendencies that influence everyday investors. Being aware of these influences can make it less likely that you will succumb to them.

Investor's Checklist

► Identifying and recognizing your own potential psychological tendencies can help you make better investment decisions.

► Overconfidence can lead to active trading, which hampers returns.

► Selective memory, cognitive dissonance, representativeness, and self-handicapping can all cause us to downplay poor-performing investments, squandering the opportunity to learn from mistakes.

► Loss aversion may cause us to focus more on our losers than our winners.

► Anchoring is when we base our decisions on something we know or believe to be important. Remember, what you paid for a stock or the recent performance of a stock are irrelevant data points when trying to figure the intrinsic value of a company.

► Money is money, whether it came from earnings or capital gains.

► Herding is taking comfort in investing with a crowd. Thinking independently and taking advantage of the market's tumultuous ways is a better way to invest.

Quiz

1   What does overconfidence in investing often lead to?

a	Rapid trading.
b	An unwillingness to part with laggard investments.
c	Focusing on only one dimension of total return.

Answers to this quiz can be found on page 175

2   What does anchoring often lead to?

a	Focusing on only one dimension of total return.
b	An unwillingness to part with laggard investments.
c	Following a market guru.

3   What does representativeness lead to?

a	Focusing on only one dimension of total return.
b	Giving too much weight to recent performance.
c	Following a market guru.

4   What does regret often lead to?

a	Making a bad sell decision because you've confused a bad outcome with a bad decision.
b	Following a market guru.
c	Focusing on only one dimension of total return.

5   What does investing with the crowd often lead to?

a	Focusing on only one dimension of total return.
b	An unwillingness to part with laggard investments.
c	Choosing investments that are inappropriate for your goals.

Worksheet

Answers to this worksheet can be found on page 184

1   Why would having a balance of credit card debt with a high interest rate while also putting money into savings, possibly at a low rate, be an example of mental accounting?

2   How might self-handicapping come into play when considering an investment that has a lot of upside potential as well as risk?

3   Consider a case in which utility stocks have performed extremely well over the past several years. What might a tendency toward holding a large percentage of utilities indicate?

4   When we set out to prove something we already believe to be true, we may be susceptible to confirmation bias. What might be a good example of this?

Lesson 303: The Case for Dividends

"A cow for her milk, / A hen for her eggs,
And a stock, by heck, / For her dividends.
An orchard for fruit, / Bees for their honey,
And stocks, besides, / For their dividends."
—*John Burr Williams*

If you've made it this far in this workbook series, you can't have escaped the following: A stock represents an ownership in a business. So let's say we are part owners as well as managers of a business, and when we closed the books on the year, our firm made a $10 million profit. Better yet, we collected all of it in cash. Now the rub—what to do with that cash?

Assuming we don't simply leave it in the corporate checkbook (though some companies certainly do), we've got four choices. We could:

▸ Reinvest it in the business
▸ Acquire another company
▸ Pay down debt
▸ Return the cash to shareholders

Real-life boards of directors face this decision in every quarter of every year. While the first three options can be productive uses for cash, the fourth—a reward to shareholders—is a critical part of the investment process. After all, why else would you want to own a stock if you never received a payback on your investment? Stocks are perpetual-life securities—there's no guaranteed payoff at some maturity date like there is with a bond.

In fact, the grandfather of security valuation (a little-known figure named John Burr Williams) defined a stock's value as the present value of future dividends. It's pretty easy to see why this is true. Even though capital gains loom large in most investors' minds, the ability to sell a stock tomorrow for more than was paid today is contingent on that stock eventually returning cash to its owner, whoever that owner might be at the time.

Dividends: The New Fad?

The two components to total return—dividends and capital gains—have two totally different tax treatments. Dividends are immediately taxable. Taxes on capital gains, on the other hand, aren't due until the stock is sold, creating a tax deferral that aids in wealth accumulation. In theory, if the dividend hadn't been declared, the value of that payment would have continued to compound tax-deferred within the company.

This natural, if not downright unavoidable, advantage that capital gains held over dividends was strengthened further by tax policies that favored capital gains over income. For years capital gains had been taxed at only half the rate of regular income, which includes wages, bonuses, interest, and (sadly) dividends. For example, in a tax cut passed in 1997, the rate levied against capital gains was capped at 19.8%, while dividends continued to be taxed at rates up to 39.6%. Some wondered why a company would pay dividends at all.

In time, investors and corporate managers responded to the tax incentives and disincentives. With the birth of a new bull market in the early 1980s, dividends came to figure less and less in investors' selection of stocks. Growth, not stability and income, earned a premium valuation, so corporate managers' incentives were to grow earnings (by reinvesting) or, at the very least, buy back stock and thereby grow earnings per share. From the bear's nadir in August 1982 to the bull's peak in August 2000, the S&P 500 rose at a 14.7% annual clip, but dividends gained at only 4.6%. The yield of the market collapsed from over 5% to just over 1%.

The reported dividend rate or yield is not always representative of what you can expect, particularly for irregular dividends or those paid by foreign companies. Always check the dividend record over at least the previous 12 months to make sure that payments aren't being double counted or that an unrepresentative payment isn't annualized—these are common problems found on financial Web sites.

Dividend? Which Dividend?

In pursuit of growth, however, a lot of businesses allocated capital poorly. The most profitable—and least risky—growth opportunities are those that are well protected by a company's economic moat. Take Hewlett-Packard, for example. For half a century it was absolutely dominant in scientific instrumentation and, as an outgrowth of that, computer printers. These markets were never going to double the size of the company overnight, but they had the potential to grow faster than the economy while throwing off huge profits and cash flow.

But H-P didn't stop with printers. The firm took its excess cash and started a consulting business, got into PCs and servers, and bought Compaq (and with Compaq inherited the remains of Digital Equipment, essentially picking up two of the technology industry's biggest losers with a single stroke). Meanwhile it spun off its instrumentation business—the company's heart and soul—as Agilent Technologies. Tens of billions of dollars invested outside its moat were eventually destroyed by competitors, not received by its shareholders.

Lots of companies are capable of investing within their existing moats, nurturing their core competencies. But the area (size of the business) surrounded by the moat grows only so fast each year, and supporting this growth will typically absorb only a modest portion of annual earnings.

Relatively few managers prove to be as good at handling the cash left over. The CEO thinks: "If we're this smart when we invest $100 million a year, think how much smarter we'll look if we invest $1 billion!" Earth to CEO: No, you won't. The additional cash would be much better off with shareholders, who could then allocate their capital among all sorts of different businesses, not just whatever the company saw as worthy of investment. But with the tax policy stacked against the payment of dividends and investors demanding growth in any and all possible forms, earnings that should have been paid out were retained, and the money was inevitably wasted.

After the bubble popped in 2000, however, investors' attention returned to capital allocation and the importance of dividends. Plus, today, the perverse incentive that double-taxing dividends (first as corporate income taxes, then as personal taxes) created for corporate managers is on hiatus due to recent tax-relief legislation. Dividend yields—just under 2% as of this writing—are still low by historical standards, but dividends seem fated to play a much larger role in market returns in the years to come.

Aren't All Dividends "Special"?

Faced with an accumulation of excess cash or an extraordinarily good profit year, a company may declare a "special" dividend. Microsoft made headlines worldwide with a one-time, $3 per share dividend in December 2004; some companies, like cyclical truck builder PACCAR, make special payouts of varying amounts on a relatively regular basis. While these payments represent a nice bonus for owning the stock, most special dividends like Microsoft's are one-off events. In other words, a special payment usually represents a one-for-one trade-off in the value of the stock, which is to say the stock usually drops by the amount of the dividend, so you wouldn't want to own the stock solely in anticipation of special payouts.

Dividends and Total Returns

During the bull market, the pursuit of rapidly growing businesses obscured the real nature of equity returns. But growth isn't all there is to successful investing; it's just one piece of a larger puzzle.

Total return includes not only price appreciation, but income as well. And what causes price appreciation? In strictly theoretical terms, there's only one answer: anticipated dividends. Earnings are just a proxy for dividend-paying power. And dividend potential is not solely driven by growth of the underlying business—in fact, rapid growth in certain capital-intensive businesses can actually be a drag on dividend prospects.

Investors who focus only on sales or earnings growth—or even just the appreciation of the stock price—stand to miss the big picture. In fact, a company that isn't paying a healthy dividend may be setting its shareholders up for an unfortunate fate.

In Jeremy Siegel's *The Future for Investors*, the market's top professor analyzed the returns of the original s&p 500 companies from the formation of the index in 1957 through the end of 2003. What was the best-performing stock? Was it in color televisions (remember Zenith)? Telecommunications (AT&T)? Groundbreaking pharmaceuticals (Syntex/Roche)? Surely, it must have been a computer stock (IBM)?

None of the above. The best of the best hails not from a hot, rapidly growing industry, but instead from a field that was actually surrendering customers the entire time: cigarette maker Philip Morris, now known as Altria Group. Over Siegel's 46-year time frame, Philip Morris posted total returns of an incredible 19.75% per year.

What was the secret? Credit a one-two punch of high dividends and profitable, moat-protected growth. Philip Morris made some acquisitions over the years, which were generally successful—but the overwhelming majority of its free cash flow was paid out as dividends or used to repurchase shares. As Marlboro gained market share and raised prices, Philip Morris grew the core business at a decent (if uninspiring) rate over the years. But what if the company—listening to the fans of growth and the foes of taxes—attempted to grow the entire business at 19.75% per year? At that rate it would have subsumed the entire U.S. economy by now.

The lesson is that no business can grow faster than the economy indefinitely, but that lack of growth doesn't cap investor returns. Amazingly, by maximizing boring old dividends and share buybacks, a low-growth business turns out to be the highest total return investment of all time. As Siegel makes abundantly clear, "growth does not equal return." Only profitable growth—in businesses protected by an economic moat—can do that.

About DRIPs

"DRIP" is common shorthand for "dividend reinvestment plan." Not every investor needs dividends for income, so many dividend-paying companies offer the option of automatically reinvesting dividends in additional shares. Signing up for DRIPs may help you focus on a company's long-term business prospects (because you will presumably participate in a DRIP for a long time), and it also allows investors to benefit from dollar-cost averaging. Many plans even offer a discount to the market price of the shares on the payment date. You can find out more about a company's DRIP by visiting the investor relations section of its Web site; you can also find out whether a company offers a DRIP or not on Morningstar.com.

Participating in a company's DRIP requires having the shares registered in your name (rather than "street name," where your broker is listed as the owner on your behalf), but before starting the paperwork to retitle your stock holdings, you'll want to find out if your broker offers a low-cost or free dividend reinvestment option as well—many of the larger firms do.

The Dividend Drill

Breaking total return into current yield and expected dividend growth, we should also sort the growth potential into two buckets—growth in the company's core business (assuming it's profitable growth, that is, or all bets are off) and the growth funded by any remaining free cash flows. We'll call this three-part process the Dividend Drill.

1. Consider the Current Dividend.

If we can establish that a stock's current dividend is sustainable long term, we can take the stock's current yield and, voila, one chunk of our total return is accounted for.

Taking a dividend for granted means establishing long-term sustainability. Nothing lasts forever—just ask the shareholders of once-venerable Goodyear Tire—although a few stocks, such as General Electric, have dividend records that come awfully close to immortality.

What establishes a secure dividend? Look for manageable debt levels. Remember, bondholders and banks are ahead of stockholders in the pay line. Next look for a reasonable payout ratio, or dividends as a percentage of profits. A payout ratio less than 80% is a good rule of thumb. Finally, look for steady cash flows. Also demand an economic moat: No-moat companies tend to be cyclical (think autos and chemicals) and lack the pricing power to maintain earnings during the inevitable industry downturns.

Coca-Cola is a good example. Right now, in mid-2005, the shares are changing hands at about $45 while paying a $1.10 annual dividend. At this time, the payout ratio is reasonable (52% over the previous 12 months), cash actually exceeds debt (no debt worries), and operating cash flows are consistent. Best of all, the moat is very wide—Coke is arguably the most valuable brand name on earth, quite the achievement for what is, after all, caramel-colored sugar water.

Coke's yield at this point is 2.4%, giving us the first building block of prospective total return. And based on current earnings power of roughly $2.00 per share, we'll have $0.90 in retained earnings to fund dividend growth, which, as noted earlier, takes two forms.

2. Assess the Company's Core Growth Potential.

One key to this analysis is understanding how much investment is required to fund this growth. Few areas of the market are bursting at the seams, but most companies and industries have at least some growth potential over time as the U.S. economy expands (figure 3%-4% per year plus inflation) and emerging markets open up. Inflation can be a tailwind, too—though taking price increases for granted with manufacturing-oriented firms is not necessarily a good idea. Fortunately for most mature businesses, supporting this baseline level of growth is relatively inexpensive, and therefore high return.

Another and often simpler way to think about the cost of growth is to look at the company's free cash flow as a percent of net income. Since free cash flow includes the cost of capital investments that support growth initiatives, the difference between earnings and free cash gives us a sense of the cost of growth.

For example, let's say free cash flow consistently totals about 60% of net income, while sales and profit growth run about 6%. This suggests that only 40% of earnings will support this growth, leaving the other 60% of net income available for dividends, debt reduction, share buybacks, and other noncore investments.

This core growth gives us the second chunk of our total return equation. For Coca-Cola, let's assume 5.2% growth in operating income over the next five years, and that Coke's growth will fall significantly below that figure thereafter. Assuming that management maintains the current payout ratio, the firm's total dividend payout should rise at a similar clip. So we bolt on this 5.2% growth to our prospective total return, bringing our expectations (including the 2.4% yield noted above) to 7.6%.

But we've got one more task before moving on to the third and final step—how much will achieving this 5.2% growth cost? One of the simplest angles is to take the growth we expect (5.2%) and divide that by a representative return on equity (a nifty 30.8% for Coke in the past five years). The resulting ratio—call it "R-cubed" for "required retention ratio"—is the proportion of earnings used to fund core growth. For Coke, the R3 is 17% of income, or $0.34 per share.

Aftertax return on invested capital is also worth a look. ROIC is actually the purest way of analyzing the incremental cost of growth; in our formula ROIC replaces return on equity in the calculation of R3. However, ROIC is more complex to use, and it leaves out the company's capital structure (mix of additional borrowings and retained earnings) that is reflected in ROE. If the capital structure is stable and returns on equity are consistent—Coke checks out here on both counts—ROE is a good metric to use.

We'll stick with ROE R3, and estimate 5.2% annual growth will cost Coke $0.34 per share. Over time, the absolute number will grow, but the proportion (17%) will remain the same as long as its two factors—growth and return on equity—stay the same.

Two-thirds of the way through our analysis, we're up to a 7.6% return, and we still have $0.56 per share to spare ($2.00 in earnings less $1.10 for the dividend and $0.34 to fund core growth). So what's the final $0.56 per share worth?

3. Evaluate the "Excess" Earnings.

After paying dividends and funding core growth, a company may have cash left over. It could opt to pay down debt, which would reduce interest expense and thus increase earnings. It might make an acquisition or some other investment, though the returns here could be spotty. Finally, it might opt to buy back stock.

Whatever the company decides to do with these excess funds, we put the result into the growth bucket of our prospective total return. In other words, we assume that any cash not used for a dividend is employed to create earnings and dividend growth. To get a proxy for the added growth potential of remaining earnings, we'll make an additional assumption that the path of least resistance is a share buyback.

This assumption is meant to err on the side of conservatism. The earnings yield (the inverse of P/E) on most stocks is generally much less than a company's return on equity, so we're not projecting much bang for this last slice of our buck. And acquisitions—returns of cash to someone else's shareholders—tend not to be priced for returns equal to existing investments.

Share buybacks boost earnings growth—EPS grows not only when the numerator (profit) expands, but also when the denominator (shares outstanding) shrinks. Dividing the excess earnings into the stock price gives us an "excess earnings yield," the third component of our total return calculation. So if Coke uses the last $0.56 of per-share earnings to repurchase stock, it will be able to retire 1.2% of its shares in the first year ($0.56 divided by a $45 share price). That, in turn, gives next year's earnings per share a 1.2% tailwind—even if earnings are flat, fewer shares outstanding mean higher earnings per share.

Sustainable Growth and Actual Growth

There are similarities between our three-part Dividend Drill and a statistic called sustainable growth. The sustainable growth ratio is (return on equity x (1 − payout ratio)) and is a proxy for how fast earnings would expand assuming 1) the firm has reinvestment opportunities for all of its retained earnings, and 2) those opportunities all have the same return potential as existing investments do.

Coke's sustainable growth rate is 30.8% x (1 − 0.53), or 14.5%. If Coke could invest all of its retained earnings at a 30.8% return, earnings would grow 14.5% indefinitely. That'd be great, but consider how high a number 14.5% really is. At that growth rate, Coca-Cola, whose global sales currently are 0.18% the size of U.S. GDP, would surpass the size of the American economy in the year 2081. While this observation testifies to the power of compound interest, it's hardly a likely outcome. The Dividend Drill thus bridges the gap between sustainable growth and actual growth.

So What's It Worth?

Totaling Coke's yield (2.4%), profit growth (5.2%), and excess earnings yield (1.2%) produces an expected total return of 8.8%. It's important to note that this total return projection is contingent on the current stock price—we can expect an 8.8% annual return from Coke only if we acquire the shares at $45. If we pay less, our total return will be higher, and vice versa.

For example, let's say the market hits the proverbial banana peel and Coke is offered at $35. Meanwhile our expectations (current earnings, dividend rate, future growth) haven't changed. Our core growth projection (5.2%) remains, but our two other factors are contingent on the stock price: At $35 the stock will yield 3.1% and our excess earnings quotient will rise to 1.6%. Our expected total return is now 9.9%, more than a full point higher. Conversely, if we wind up paying $55, our total return prospects are substantially reduced. Coke's yield will fall to 2%, the excess earnings quotient to 1.1%, and our expected return to 8.3%.

This analysis essentially calculates fair value in reverse—instead of using a required rate of return to yield a fair price for the stock, we use the stock price to calculate the shares' total return. Coke's fair value is the price at which its total return is equal to the return we would require for any stock of similar risk characteristics. Morningstar's fair value estimate in mid-2005 for Coke was $54, which was calculated using an 8.5% cost of equity—a return virtually identical to our total return projection if we use $54 as the stock's price.

What's the "right" required rate of return? Unfortunately there's more art than science to this, but we have two observations. First, over a very long period of time (200 years), the market has managed to return something around 10%. Lower-risk stocks would offer less, while higher-risk situations should require more. But most established, dividend-paying companies would fall in a range between 8% and 12%. Whatever you determine a "fair" return to be, demand more. This way you have a margin of safety between your assumptions and subsequent realities.

Using the Dividend Drill

This analysis is not suited to every stock or situation. For one thing, even with the surge in the popularity of dividends in recent years, less than half of U.S. stocks pay a dividend. It's also not particularly well suited to deeply cyclical firms, whose earnings power and even dividend rates will vary widely from year to year. It's also not suited for emerging-growth stories. But for the ranks of relatively consistent, mature, moat-protected stocks—of which there are hundreds, if not thousands, to pick from—we can use the dividend as a critical selection tool.

The Bottom Line

Tradition-minded investors like us are glad to see dividends making a comeback. Compared with retained earnings or buybacks, a solid dividend establishes a firm intrinsic value for the stock, helps reduce the stock's volatility, and acts as a check on management's capital-allocation practices. Simply put, it's the way things were meant to be. And using the basic tools described in this lesson, you can use the dividend to identify high-quality stocks with good total return prospects.

Investor's Checklist

▶ Dividends and dividend growth provide a solid basis for a stock's intrinsic value. In the end, a stock will only be worth the value of the dividends it pays.

▶ Numerous academic studies have established the importance of dividends and dividend reinvestment in investor returns. In some studies, dividends accounted for more than half of long-term total returns.

▶ Dividends are making a comeback. The yield on the S&P 500 is still below historic norms at just under 2%, but real dividend growth (adjusted for inflation) is running at its best pace in decades.

▶ Dividends are now taxed on an equal footing with capital gains.

▶ In addition to the role a dividend plays in returns, it's a simple and versatile analytic tool.

Quiz

Answers to this quiz can be found on page 176

1 Given a quarterly dividend of $0.30 per share and a $27 stock price, what is the yield?

a	1.1%.
b	4.4%.
c	I need to know the company's ROE first.

2 Amalgamated Widget has a payout ratio of 87%. This may indicate any of the following, except:

a	87% of dividends are guaranteed.
b	Earnings are artificially depressed.
c	The company has few reinvestment opportunities.

3 What does the sustainable growth ratio tell you about a stock's prospects?

a	A definitive growth rate of future dividends.
b	The availability of attractive investment opportunities.
c	How fast the company could grow at its current return on equity, given sufficient investment opportunities.

4 Why is an economic moat important for a dividend-paying firm?

a	It protects the company's earnings (and dividend-paying power) from competitive pressures.
b	It implies the company has investment opportunities that will allow it to grow the dividend.
c	Both of the above.

5 According to Jeremy Siegel, what was the top-performing stock between 1957 and 2003?

a	A computer company.
b	A tobacco company.
c	An automobile company.

Worksheet

Here is some information about fictional company Peter's Monster Trucks.

Answers to this worksheet can be found on page 184

Stock Price: $36.00
Earnings Per Share: $2.25
Dividend Per Share: $1.40
Return on Equity: 14%

1   What is the company's payout ratio?

2   What is the firm's sustainable growth rate?

3   Calculate the required retention ratio (R3) if we expect the business to grow at a 3% rate.

4   How much would it cost (per share) for Peter's to grow at this 3%?

5   What is the excess earnings yield for Peter's?

6   Calculate the stock's total return potential assuming a business growth rate of 3%.

7   Would you buy this stock?

Lesson 304: 20 Stock-Investing Tips

"The question is not what you look at, but what you see."—Henry David Thoreau

Here at Morningstar, our stock analyst staff has nearly a thousand years of collective investment experience. In this chapter, we've boiled down some of our most salient observations into 20 suggestions we think will make you a better stock investor.

1. Keep It Simple.

Keeping it simple in investing is not stupid. Seventeenth-century philosopher Blaise Pascal once said, "All man's miseries derive from not being able to sit quietly in a room alone." This aptly describes the investing process.

Those who trade too often, focus on irrelevant data points, or try to predict the unpredictable are likely to encounter some unpleasant surprises when investing. By keeping it simple—focusing on companies with economic moats, requiring a margin of safety when buying, and investing with a long-term horizon—you can greatly enhance your odds of success.

2. Have the Proper Expectations.

Are you getting into stocks with the expectation that quick riches soon await? Hate to be a wet blanket, but unless you are extremely lucky, you will not double your money in the next year investing in stocks. Such returns generally cannot be achieved unless you take on a great deal of risk by, for instance, buying extensively on margin or taking a flier on a chancy security. At this point, you have crossed the line from investing into speculating.

Though stocks have historically been the highest-return asset class, this still means returns in the 10%-12% range. These returns have also come with a great deal of volatility. (See Lesson 103 of Workbook #1 for more.) If you don't have the proper expectations for the returns and volatility you will experience when investing in stocks, irrational behavior—taking on exorbitant risk in get-rich-quick strategies, trading too much, swearing off stocks forever because of a short-term loss—may ensue.

3. Be Prepared to Hold for a Long Time.

In the short term, stocks tend to be volatile, bouncing around every which way on the back of Mr. Market's knee-jerk reactions to news as it hits. (Much more on Mr. Market is in coming lessons.) Trying to predict the market's short-term movements is not only impossible, it's maddening. It is helpful to remember what Benjamin Graham said: In the short run, the market is like a voting machine—tallying up which firms are popular and unpopular. But in the long run, the market is like a weighing machine—assessing the substance of a company.

Yet all too many investors are still focused on the popularity contests that happen every day, and then grow frustrated as the stocks of their companies—which may have sound and growing businesses—do not move. Be patient, and keep your focus on a company's fundamental performance. In time, the market will recognize and properly value the cash flows that your businesses produce.

4. Tune Out the Noise.

There are many media outlets competing for investors' attention, and most of them center on presenting and justifying daily price movements of various markets. This means lots of prices—stock prices, oil prices, money prices, frozen orange juice concentrate prices—accompanied by lots of guesses about why prices changed. Unfortunately, the price changes rarely represent any real change in value. Rather, they merely represent volatility, which is inherent to any open market. Tuning out this noise will not only give you more time, it will help you focus on what's important to your investing success—the performance of the companies you own.

Likewise, just as you won't become a better baseball player by just staring at statistical sheets, your investing skills will not improve by only looking at stock prices or charts. Athletes improve by practicing and hitting the gym; investors improve by getting to know more about their companies and the world around them.

5. Behave Like an Owner.

We'll say it again—stocks are not merely things to be traded, they represent ownership interests in companies. If you are buying businesses, it makes sense to act like a business owner. This means reading and analyzing financial statements on a regular basis, weighing the competitive strengths of businesses, making predictions about future trends, as well as having conviction and not acting impulsively.

6. Buy Low, Sell High.

If you let stock prices alone guide your buy and sell decisions, you are letting the tail wag the dog. It's frightening how many people will buy stocks just because they've recently risen, and those same people will sell when stocks have recently performed poorly. Wake-up call: When stocks have fallen, they are low, and that is generally the time to buy! Similarly, when they have skyrocketed, they are high, and that is generally the time to sell! Don't let fear (when stocks have fallen) or greed (when stocks have risen) take over your decision making.

7. Watch Where You Anchor.

If you read the earlier lesson on behavioral finance, you are familiar with the concept of anchoring, or mentally clinging to a specific reference point. Unfortunately, many people anchor on the price they paid for a stock, and gauge their own performance (and that of their companies) relative to this number.

Remember, stocks are priced and eventually weighed on the estimated value of future cash flows businesses will produce. Focus on this. If you focus on what you paid for a stock, you are focused on an irrelevant data point from the past. Be careful where you place your anchors.

8. Remember that Economics Usually Trumps Management Competence.

You can be a great racecar driver, but if your car only has half the horsepower as the rest of the field, you are not going to win. Likewise, the best skipper in the world will not be able to effectively guide a ship across the ocean if the hull has a hole and the rudder is broken.

Also keep in mind that management can (for better or for worse) change quickly, while the economics of a business are usually much more static. Given the choice between a wide-moat, cash-cow business with mediocre management and a no-moat, terrible-return businesses with bright management, take the former.

9. Be Careful of Snakes.

Though the economics of a business are key, the stewards of a company's capital are still important. Even wide-moat businesses can be poor investments if snakes are in control. If you find a company that has management practices or compensation that makes your stomach turn, watch out.

When weighing management, it is helpful to remember the parable of the snake. Late one winter evening, a man came across a snake on the path. The snake asked, "Will you please help me, sir? I am cold, hungry and will surely die if left alone." The man replied, "But you are a snake, and you will surely bite me!" The snake replied, "Please, I am desperate, and I promise not to bite you."

So the man thought about it, and decided to take the snake home. The man warmed the snake up by the fire and prepared some food for the snake. After they enjoyed a meal together, the snake suddenly bit the man. The man asked, "Why did you bite me? I saved your life and showed you much generosity!" The snake simply replied, "You knew I was a snake when you picked me up."

Morningstar.com Premium Members have access to Stewardship Grades and commentary on management for nearly all of the approximately 1,600 companies we currently cover.

Stewardship Grades

10. Bear in Mind that Past Trends Often Continue.

One of the most often heard disclaimers in the financial world is, "Past performance is no guarantee of future results." While this is indeed true, past performance is still a pretty darn good indicator of how people will perform again in the future. This applies not just to investment managers, but company managers as well. Great managers often find new business opportunities in unexpected places. If a company has a strong record of entering and profitably expanding new lines of business, make sure to consider this when valuing the firm. Don't be afraid to stick with winning managers.

11. Prepare for the Situation to Proceed Faster than You Think.

Most deteriorating businesses will do so faster than you anticipate. Be very wary of value traps, or companies that look cheap but are generating little or no economic value. On the other hand, strong businesses with solid competitive advantages will often exceed your expectations. Have a very wide margin of safety with a troubled business, but do not be afraid to have a much smaller margin of safety for a wonderful business with a shareholder-friendly management team.

12. Expect Surprises to Repeat.

The first big positive surprise from a company is unlikely to be the last. Ditto the first big negative surprise. Remember the "cockroach theory." Namely, the first cockroach you see is probably not the only one around; there are likely scores more that you can't see.

13. Don't Be Stubborn.

David St. Hubbins memorably said in the movie *This is Spinal Tap*, "It's such a fine line between stupid and clever." In investing, the line between being patient and being stubborn is even finer, unfortunately.

Patience comes from watching companies rather than stock prices, and letting your investment theses play out. If a stock you recently bought has fallen, but nothing has changed with the company, patience will likely pay off. However, if you find yourself constantly discounting bad news or downplaying the importance of deteriorating financials, you might be crossing that fine line into stubborn territory. Being stubborn in investing can be expensive.

Always ask yourself, "What is this business worth now? If I didn't already own it, would I buy it today?" Honestly and correctly answering these questions will not only help you be patient when patience is needed, but it will also greatly help you with your selling decisions.

14. Listen to Your Gut.

Any valuation model you may create for a company is only as good as the assumptions about the future that are put into it. If the output of a model does not make sense, then it's worthwhile to double-check your projections and calculations. Use DCF valuation models (or any other valuation models) as guides, not oracles.

15. Know Your Friends, and Your Enemies.

What's the short interest in a stock you are interested in? What mutual funds own the company, and what is the record of those fund managers? Does company management have "skin in the game" via a meaningful ownership stake? Have company insiders been selling or buying? At the margin, these are valuable pieces of collateral evidence for your investment thesis on a company.

16. Recognize the Signs of a Top.

Whether it is tulip bulbs in 17th-century Holland, gold in 1849, or Beanie Babies and Internet stocks in the 1990s, any time a crowd has unanimously agreed that a certain investment is a "can't lose" opportunity, you are probably best off to avoid that investment. The tide is likely to turn soon. Also, when you see people making investments that they have no business making (think bellboys giving tips on bonds, auto mechanics day-trading stocks in their shops, or successful doctors giving up medicine to "flip" real estate), that's also a sign to search for the exits.

17. Look for Quality.

If you focus your attention on companies that have wide economic moats, you will find firms that are virtually certain to have higher earnings 5 or 10 years from now. You want to make sure that you focus your attention on companies that increase the intrinsic value of their shares over time. These afford you the luxury of being patient and holding for a long time. Otherwise, you are just playing a game of chicken with the stock market.

18. Don't Buy Without Value.

The difference between a great company and a great investment is the price you pay. There were many fantastic businesses around in 2000, but very few of them were attractively priced at the time. Finding great companies is only half the equation in picking stocks; figuring out an appropriate price to pay is just as important to your investment success.

19. Always Have a Margin of Safety.

Unless you unlock the secret to time-travel, you will never escape the inherent unpredictability of the future. This is why it is key to always have a margin of safety built in to any stock purchase you may make—you will be partially protected if your projections about the future don't exactly pan out the way you expected.

You will also see in coming lessons that having a margin of safety is a recurring theme among several great investors. This is no accident; margin of safety really is that important.

20. Think Independently.

Another common characteristic you will find in the next section is that great investors are willing to go against the grain. You should find zero comfort in relying on the advice of others and putting your money where everyone else is investing. Quite simply, it pays to go against the crowd because the crowd is often wrong.

Also remember that successful investing is more about having the proper temperament than it is about having exceptional intelligence. If you can keep your head while everyone else is losing theirs, you will be well ahead of the game—able to buy at the bottom, and sell at the top.

The Bottom Line

We've distilled a lot of information and collective wisdom into these 20 tips, most of which we have touched on in greater depth elsewhere in this series of workbooks. We firmly believe that if you heed the advice contained here, you will make better decisions when buying and selling your stocks.

Investor's Checklist

▶ Our 20 tips in this lesson are:

1. Keep it simple.
2. Have the proper expectations.
3. Be prepared to hold for a long time.
4. Tune out the noise.
5. Behave like an owner.
6. Buy low, sell high.
7. Watch where you anchor.
8. Remember that economics usually trump management competence.
9. Be careful of snakes.
10. Bear in mind that past trends often continue.
11. Prepare for the situation to proceed faster than you may think.
12. Expect surprises to repeat.
13. Don't be stubborn.
14. Listen to your gut.
15. Know your friends, and your enemies.
16. Recognize the signs of a top.
17. Look for quality.
18. Don't buy without value.
19. Always have a margin of safety.
20. Think independently.

Quiz

Answers to this quiz can be found on page 177

1   All else equal, you should be most interested in buying:

a	A wide-moat company with mediocre management.
b	A no-moat company with highly educated management.
c	A company with significant insider selling.

2   Which of these sayings would Morningstar most disagree with?

a	"It's a fine line between being patient and stubborn."
b	"There is no correlation between past performance and future results."
c	"Keeping it simple is not stupid."

3   Which of the following should you tune out?

a	Whether company management owns stock or not.
b	A prediction on television about where the market will be next year.
c	Performance of a company's new product.

4   Which of the following is not a common characteristic of great investors?

a	Ability to predict short-term market movements.
b	Willingness to go against the crowd.
c	Requiring a margin of safety.

5   Which of the following activities is most likely to improve your investing skills?

a	Carefully accounting for your portfolio's unrealized capital gains and losses.
b	Checking stock quotes hourly.
c	Reading one of your company's annual reports.

Worksheet

1   Name three examples of data points that are irrelevant to a company's future cash flow:

Answers to this worksheet can be found on page 186

1.

2.

3.

2   Decide if the following phrases are more likely to be "right" or "wrong" in investing:

	Right	Wrong
"Going with the crowd is okay. If most people are buying something, they must know something I don't."	○	○
"The economics of a business do not matter as long as management is highly educated."	○	○
"Even a company with an attractive business should be avoided if snakes are in charge."	○	○
"Past performance of management should never be considered because it is of no relevance to future performance."	○	○
"You don't need a margin of safety if you are buying a company with a wide moat and excellent management."	○	○
"Fear and greed can negatively impact your investment decision making."	○	○
"It is a good thing when company management has a significant ownership stake in the firm they are running."	○	○
"Quality companies can be purchased at any price."	○	○

Strategies of the Greats

Lesson 305: Deep Value—Benjamin Graham

"An investment operation is one which, upon thorough analysis, promises safety of principal and an adequate return. Operations not meeting these requirements are speculative."—Benjamin Graham

Benjamin Graham taught an investment class at the Columbia University business school for 28 years. If you had been a student in Graham's classes during the early 1950s, your textbook, *Security Analysis*, would have been written by Graham himself, along with David Dodd.

You may also have met a few interesting students by the names of Warren Buffett, Bill Ruane, Tom Knapp, and Walter Schloss. Each of these men would go on to manage investments in one form or another. Buffett and Schloss both started investment partnerships. Buffett folded his partnership in 1969, but his partners were given the opportunity to receive shares of a struggling textile manufacturer named Berkshire Hathaway.

Ruane and Knapp started firms that manage public mutual funds. In 1984, Buffett returned to Columbia to give a speech commemorating the 50th anniversary of the publication of *Security Analysis*. During that speech, he presented his own investment record as well as those of Ruane, Knapp, and Schloss:

	Years	Return	Benchmark Return
Buffett Partnership Ltd.	1957 - 1969	2,794.9%	152.6% (Dow Jones)
Schloss Partnership	1956 - 1984	23,104.7%	887.2% (S&P 500)
Tweedy, Browne Inc. (Knapp)	1968 - 1983	1,661.2%	238.5% (S&P 500)
Sequoia Fund Inc. (Ruane)	1970 - 1984	775.3%	270.0% (S&P 500)

As you can see, each of these men posted investment results that blew away the returns of the overall market. (The speech was aptly titled "The Super-investors of Graham-and-Doddsville.") Buffett noted that each of the portfolios varied greatly in the number and type of stocks, but what did not vary was the managers' adherence to Graham's investment principles. The investment principles taught by Graham at Columbia served his students exceptionally well, and it is difficult to overstate the influence Graham had on the field of professional stock analysis. The good news is that Graham made the same principles easily accessible for ordinary investors by writing the classic book *The Intelligent Investor*.

Graham-Newman Corporation	Graham was not only a preeminent teacher and author, but also an extraordinary investor. When Graham graduated from Columbia in 1914, the university offered him three different teaching positions in the English, math, and philosophy departments. Graham, instead, headed to Wall Street where he began by recording stock prices on a chalkboard for $12 per week. Before long, however, he was successfully managing a small investment firm, but he was nearly wiped out by the crashes of 1929 and 1932. Graham eventually recovered and with his partner Jerome Newman founded Graham-Newman Corporation in 1936. Over the next 20 years, until Graham retired in 1956, Graham-Newman's returns averaged a remarkable 20% annually.

The Principles of Value Investing

Multibillion-dollar casinos have been built in the desert because of the insatiable human desire to speculate. However, when speculation is confused with investment, trouble inevitably follows. The Internet bubble of the late 1990s is merely the most recent example of the speculative frenzies that occasionally occur in financial markets. In *The Intelligent Investor*, Graham set forth the principles that form the foundation of value investing. Value investors seek to purchase assets at prices that are substantially below the assets' true, or intrinsic, value. Graham's timeless principles provide a map that all value investors can follow to stock market success. According to Graham, investing consists of three elements:

1. Thorough Analysis

Stocks are not merely pieces of paper or electronic quotations on a computer screen, but partial ownership interests in real businesses. Therefore, you must thoroughly analyze the underlying business and its prospects before purchasing a stock. Equally important—given the endless amount of data that flows from the stock market on a daily basis—is recognizing the information you must ignore or discard. For example, the average price of a stock over the past 50 days may be important to so-called chartists or technical analysts, but does that have any effect on the safety or value of the underlying business? As Graham wrote, you must study "the facts in light of established standards of safety and value."

2. Safety of Principal

Warren Buffett is fond of saying that his two rules of investing are Rule #1: Don't Lose Money, and Rule #2: Don't Forget Rule #1. Buffett undoubtedly inherited his strong aversion to permanent capital loss from Graham. To succeed over an investment lifetime, you do not have to find the next Microsoft or Dell, but it is necessary that you avoid significant losses.

The chart on the next page compares the return of two hypothetical investors starting with $10,000. Investor A consistently earns 5% annually, while Investor B suffers a 50% loss in the first year and then earns 10% annually afterward. As you can see, even though Investor B's return is double that of Investor A after the first year, it takes 17 years for Investor B to catch Investor A after suffering the 50% loss. Graham defined "safety of principal" as "protection against loss under all normal or reasonably likely conditions or variations." Speculators who chased the high-flying stocks of the late 1990s should have heeded Graham's advice, as many are unlikely to ever recover from the losses they endured once the bubble burst.

Rule #1: Don't Lose Money

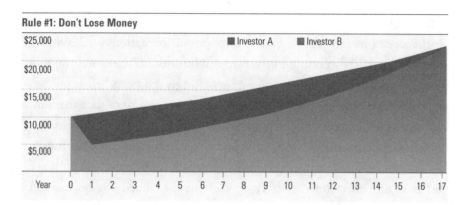

3. Adequate Return

For Graham, an "adequate" or "satisfactory" return meant "any rate or amount of return, however low, which the investor is willing to accept, provided he acts with reasonable intelligence." Many investors will find that the best way to own common stocks is through a low-cost mutual fund or ETF (exchange-traded fund) that tracks a broad market index such as the S&P 500. Index funds allow investors to participate in the growth of American business, which has been very satisfactory over the last century. In addition, very few active managers have outperformed S&P 500 index funds over long periods of time. Therefore, if you decide to construct your own portfolio of stocks or to purchase shares of an actively managed mutual fund, your investment return must exceed that of a low-cost index fund over the long term to be "adequate." Otherwise, "reasonable intelligence" should dictate that you own an index fund.

Intrinsic Value

How much should you pay for a business? Every day the stock market offers prices for thousands of businesses, but how do you know if the price for any particular business is too low or too high? To succeed as an investor, you must be able to estimate a business's true worth, or "intrinsic value."

For Graham, a business's intrinsic value could be estimated from its financial statements, namely the balance sheet and income statement. For example, in 1926 Graham discovered that Northern Pipe Line, an oil transport company, owned a collection of railroad bonds that were worth $95 for each of its shares. However, Northern's stock was selling for only $65 per share. It does not take a genius of Graham's caliber to see from Northern's balance sheet that its intrinsic value was at least $95 per share since the company also owned valuable pipeline assets. Although it took a proxy fight, Graham eventually brought Northern's management to his way of thinking: Northern sold the bonds and paid a $70 per share dividend.

A business's intrinsic value is also directly related to its earnings power, or the profits that are available to the business's owners. This valuation method, Graham wrote, consisted of "estimating the average earnings over a period of years in the future and then multiplying that estimate by an appropriate 'capitalization factor.'"

However, Graham observed two significant difficulties with this approach. First, he correctly noted that "no one really knows anything about what will happen in the distant future, but analysts and investors have strong views on the subject just the same." Predicting earnings is a task fraught with inaccuracy, and investors should be careful not to take a view that is too optimistic. Second, the determination of an appropriate "capitalization factor" or price/earnings ratio for a stock is an art, dependent on such considerations as the business's long-term prospects, management quality, financial strength and capital structure, dividend record, and current dividend rate.

As a guide, Graham offered a simple formula for estimating an appropriate price/earnings ratio, and thus a business's intrinsic value based on its earnings power.

Value ⊜ Current (Normal) Earnings ⊗ (8.5 ⊕ Twice the Expected Annual Growth Rate)

The expected growth should be the growth expected over the next 7 to 10 years.

As you can see, the faster a business is able to increase earnings, the higher its appropriate price/earnings ratio will be. The following table summarizes the appropriate price/earnings ratio at various growth rates based on Graham's formula.

Graham's P/E Ratios Versus Growth Rates

Expected Annual Growth Rate (%)	0	5	10	20
Cumulative 10-Year Growth (%)	0	63	159	319
Price/Earnings Ratio	8.5	18.5	28.5	48.5

Now that we have the price/earnings ratio, we simply multiply that number by the current earnings per share, so long as that figure represents the business's normalized earnings power and is not distorted by special charges or gains. For example, if a business earns $1 per share and is expected to grow earnings at 5% annually over the next 10 years, its intrinsic value according to Graham's simple formula is $1 \times (8.5 + 2 \times 5)$, $18.50 per share.

Another Insight from Graham's Formula

By using simple algebra, we can rearrange Graham's intrinsic value formula to find another useful application. If we know a stock's price and current earnings per share, we can use Graham's formula to calculate the expected growth that is implied in the stock price.

Expected Growth ⊖ (P/E Ratio ⊖ 8.5) ⊗ 1/2

For example, Google has current earnings of $2.53 per share and a stock price of about $300, giving it a P/E ratio of about 118. According to Graham's formula, the market is expecting Google's earnings to grow by a staggering $(118 - 8.5) \times 1/2$, or roughly 55% annually for the next 10 years.

Mr. Market

If all investors based their investment decisions on rational and conservative estimates of intrinsic value, it would be very difficult to make money in the stock market. Fortunately, the participants in the stock market are humans subject to the corroding influence of emotions. Investors are frequently given to bouts of over-optimism and greed, which causes stock prices to be bid up to very high levels. These same investors are also vulnerable to excessive pessimism and fear, in which case, stock prices are driven down substantially below intrinsic value.

Graham offers intelligent investors an escape from the swift tides of greed and fear. He wrote, "Basically, price fluctuations have only one significant meaning for the true investor. They provide him with an opportunity to buy wisely when prices fall sharply and sell wisely when they advance a great deal. At other times he will do better if he forgets about the stock market." Graham's attitude toward market fluctuations, of course, makes perfect sense. Can you imagine waiting to purchase a television until its price went up, but refusing to buy the same television when it went on sale? Strange as it seems, behavior that is blatantly irrational in most aspects of life is commonplace in the stock market.

Graham succinctly captured his liberating philosophy toward market fluctuations in the famous parable of Mr. Market. Graham said to imagine you had a partner in a private business named Mr. Market. Mr. Market, the obliging fellow that he is, shows up daily to tell you what he thinks your interest in the business is worth.

On most days, the price he quotes is reasonable and justified by the business's prospects. However, Mr. Market suffers from some rather incurable emotional problems; you see, he is very temperamental. When Mr. Market is overcome by boundless optimism or bottomless pessimism, he will quote you a price that, as Graham noted, "seems to you a little short of silly." As an intelligent investor, you should not fall under Mr. Market's influence, but rather you should learn to take advantage of him.

The value of your interest should be determined by rationally appraising the business's prospects, and you can happily sell when Mr. Market quotes you a ridiculously high price and buy when he quotes you an absurdly low price. The best part of your association with Mr. Market is that he does not care how many times you take advantage of him. No matter how many times you saddle him with losses or rob him of gains, he will arrive the next day ready to do business with you again.

The lesson behind Graham's Mr. Market parable is obvious. Every day the stock market offers investors quotes on thousands of businesses, and you are free either to ignore or take advantage of those prices. You must always remember that it is not Mr. Market's guidance you are interested in, but rather his wallet.

Margin of Safety

If you had asked Graham to distill the secret of sound investing into three words, he might have replied, "margin of safety." These are still the right three words and will remain so for as long as humans are unable to accurately predict the future.

As Graham repeatedly warned, any estimate of intrinsic value is based on numerous assumptions about the future, which are unlikely to be completely accurate. By allowing yourself a margin of safety—paying only $60 for a stock you think is worth $100, for example—you provide for errors in your forecasts and unforeseeable events that may alter the business landscape.

Just think, if you were asked to build a bridge over which 10,000-pound trucks were to pass, would you build it to hold exactly 10,000 pounds?

Of course not—you'd build the bridge to hold 15,000 or 20,000 pounds. That is your margin of safety.

The chart below illustrates the importance of following Graham's margin of safety maxim.

Paying Up Doesn't Pay Off

	1999 P/E	2004 P/E	1999 Price	2004 Price	5-Year EPS Growth	5-Year Total Return
Coca-Cola	47	20	$58	$42	66%	-28%
Pfizer	42	13	$32	$27	165%	-16%
Wal-Mart	58	23	$69	$53	93%	-23%
Dell	75	35	$51	$42	78%	-18%
Microsoft	78	21	$58	$27	69%	-53%
Intel	36	21	$41	$24	-4%	-41%
Cisco	134	24	$54	$19	100%	-65%
Average	67	22	$52	$33	81%	-35%

This chart contains seven of the best businesses in existence: the world's leading soft drink, pharmaceutical, retail, computer, software, semiconductor, and networking companies. In the five years from 1999 to 2004, these wonders of American business boosted their earnings per share by an average of 81%, yet had you invested in all of them in 1999, your aggregate return would have been a disappointing negative 35%. The cause of your loss would be the high price you paid for these businesses in 1999 when their price/earnings ratio averaged a breathtaking 67 times.

By 2004, the average price/earnings ratio had returned to a more rational 22 times, more than offsetting the spectacular gains in earnings per share posted by these corporate giants. An intelligent investor would have recognized that even for the greatest businesses in the world, at 67 times earnings, Mr. Market was asking too high a price and no margin of safety was available.

Think Independently

In a recent interview, Warren Buffett said the best advice he ever got from Graham was to think independently. Just as you should ignore Mr. Market's daily communications (unless, of course, he gives you an interesting quote), you should also derive no comfort in either standing with or against the crowd. As Graham wrote, "You are neither right nor wrong because the crowd disagrees with you. You are right because your data and reasoning are right." If you have reached a rational conclusion about a stock based on sound judgment, you should act even though others around you may hesitate or differ.

The Bottom Line

When Benjamin Graham passed away in 1976, Warren Buffett wrote this about Graham's teachings: "In an area where much looks foolish within weeks or months after publication, Ben's principles have remained sound—their value often enhanced and better understood in the wake of financial storms that demolished flimsier intellectual structures. His counsel of soundness brought unfailing rewards to his followers—even to those with natural abilities inferior to more gifted practitioners who stumbled while following counsels of brilliance or fashion." Buffett's words remain undeniably true today. Investing is most intelligent when it is most businesslike, and investors who follow Graham's principles will continue to reap rewards in the stock market.

Investor's Checklist

▶ Born in London in 1894 as Benjamin Grossbaum, Graham emigrated to the United States when he was one year old. Graham graduated from Columbia University in 1914 and was offered a teaching position in three different Columbia departments.

▶ Graham's *Security Analysis*, published in 1934, was the first book to articulate a framework for the systematic analysis of stocks and bonds. Graham later wrote *The Intelligent Investor* to bring many of the same concepts to the lay investor. Both books should be at the very top of the required reading list for serious value investors.

▶ One of Graham's must successful investments was in the automobile insurer GEICO, where he served as chairman of the board.

▶ One of Graham's favorite investment techniques was to purchase net-current-asset bargains, or net-nets. Net-nets were stocks that traded for less than the value of their current assets minus all liabilities.

▶ Graham's students, such as Warren Buffett and Bill Ruane, are among some of the best investors of the past century.

Quiz

Answers to this quiz can be found on page 177

1   Which classic investment book did Graham not author?

a	*Security Analysis.*
b	*The Intelligent Investor.*
c	*Common Stocks and Uncommon Profits.*

2   According to Graham, what must an investor do before purchasing a stock?

a	Speak with management extensively.
b	Ensure the current price allows for a margin of safety.
c	Use technical analysis to predict short-term price movements.

3   Which of the following best defines the term "intrinsic value"?

a	The highest price at which someone may purchase a stock in the future.
b	The true worth of a business, which is entirely separate from its stock market price.
c	A stock's current market price.

4   Which statement would Graham most agree with?

a	"Investing is most intelligent when it is most businesslike."
b	"A stock's price behavior over the past 30 days will tell you a lot about the business."
c	"Stocks of great companies are a good buy at any price."

5   According to Graham, what are the features of an investment operation?

a	Making high-risk, high-return bets.
b	Thorough analysis, safety of principal, and an adequate return.
c	Trading based on chart formations.

Worksheet

1   Fictional company Erika's Bookstores is expected to grow its $1 of earnings per share by
    5% annually over the next 10 years. Its stock is trading for $12.50. Using Graham's formula,
    is the stock of Erika's currently undervalued or overvalued relative to its market price?

Answers to this worksheet can be found on page 187

2   Does Erika's Bookstores' stock from the problem above offer a margin of safety at its current
    trading price?

3   Fictional company Peter Trading Associates earned $0.38 per share last year, and its stock
    trades for $32. Using Graham's formula, what growth expectations are implied by the
    stock price?

Lesson 306: Holding Superior Growth—
Philip Fisher

"If the job has been correctly done when a common stock is purchased, the time to sell it is—almost never."—Phil Fisher

The late Phil Fisher was one of the great investors of all time and the author of the classic book, *Common Stocks and Uncommon Profits*. Fisher started his money management firm, Fisher & Co., in 1931 and over the next seven decades made tremendous amounts of money for his clients. For example, he was an early investor in semiconductor giant Texas Instruments, whose market capitalization recently stood at well over $40 billion. Fisher also purchased Motorola in 1955, and in a testament to long-term investing, held the stock until his death in 2004.

Warren Buffett (our subject in the next lesson) has described his investment philosophy as "85% Ben Graham and 15% Phil Fisher." Buffett's partner, Charlie Munger, said this about Fisher at the 1993 Berkshire Hathaway annual meeting: "Phil Fisher believed in concentrating in about 10 good investments and was happy with a limited number. That is very much in our playbook. And he believed in knowing a lot about the things he did invest in. And that's in our playbook, too. And the reason why it's in our playbook is that to some extent, we learned it from him." This high praise from two very smart (and rich) investors should encourage anyone to study and learn from Fisher.

Fisher's Investment Philosophy
Fisher's investment philosophy can be summarized in a single sentence: Purchase and hold for the long term a concentrated portfolio of outstanding companies with compelling growth prospects that you understand very well. This sentence is clear on its face, but let us parse it carefully to understand the advantages of Fisher's approach.

①

Develop a Philosophy

If you are interesting in learning about how Fisher developed his investment philosophy, there is a short essay in the back of *Common Stocks and Uncommon Profits* aptly titled "Developing an Investing Philosophy."

The question that every investor faces is, of course, what to buy? Fisher's answer is to purchase the shares of superbly managed growth companies, and he devoted an entire chapter in *Common Stocks and Uncommon Profits* to this topic. The chapter begins with a comparison of "statistical bargains," or stocks that appear cheap based solely on accounting figures, and growth stocks, or stocks with excellent growth prospects based on an intelligent appraisal of the underlying business's characteristics.

The problem with statistical bargains, Fisher noted, is that while there may be some genuine bargains to be found, in many cases the businesses face daunting headwinds that cannot be discerned from accounting figures, such that in a few years the current "bargain" prices will have proved to be very high. Furthermore, Fisher stated that over a period of many years, a well-selected growth stock will substantially outperform a statistical bargain. The reason for this disparity, Fisher wrote, is that a growth stock, whose intrinsic value grows steadily over time, will tend to appreciate "hundreds of per cent each decade," while it is unusual for a statistical bargain to be "as much as 50 per cent undervalued."

Fisher divided the universe of growth stocks into large and small companies. On one end of the spectrum are large financially strong companies with solid growth prospects. At the time, these included IBM, Dow Chemical, and DuPont, all of which increased fivefold in the 10-year period from 1946 to 1956.

Although such returns are quite satisfactory, the real home runs are to be found in "small and frequently young companies...[with] products that might bring a sensational future." Of these companies, Fisher wrote, "the young growth stock offers by far the greatest possibility of gain. Sometimes this can mount up to several thousand per cent in a decade." Fisher's answer to the question of what to buy is clear: All else equal, investors with the time and inclination should concentrate their efforts on uncovering young companies with outstanding growth prospects.

As we will see next, Fisher focused much attention on qualitative attributes, which means that you won't be able to find answers simply by flipping through a company's financial statements. To uncover the business insights described in Fisher's 15 points, investors must do their research footwork, or "scuttlebutt." You should ask questions of management, competitors, suppliers, customers, and anyone else who might have useful information. As Fisher wrote, "Go to five companies in the industry, ask each of them intelligent questions about the points of strength and weakness of the other four, and nine times out of ten a surprisingly detailed and accurate picture of all five will emerge."

The Value of "Scuttlebutt"

Fisher's 15 Points—What Does a Growth Stock Look Like?

All good principles are timeless, and Fisher's famous "Fifteen Points to Look for in a Common Stock" from *Common Stocks and Uncommon Profits* remain as relevant today as when they were first published. The 15 points are a qualitative guide to finding superbly managed companies with excellent growth prospects. According to Fisher, a company must qualify on most of these 15 points to be considered a worthwhile investment:

1. Does the company have products or services with sufficient market potential to make possible a sizable increase in sales for at least several years?

A company seeking a sustained period of spectacular growth must have products that address large and expanding markets. For example, Dell Computer was one of the great growth stocks of the 1990s because the market for personal computers was growing rapidly and was potentially very large. On the other hand, if you were to examine the television set market, you could have easily seen there was not much potential for growth because nearly all households in the United States already had televisions.

2. Does the management have a determination to continue to develop products or processes that will still further increase total sales potentials when the growth potentials of currently attractive product lines have largely been exploited?

All markets eventually mature, and to maintain above-average growth over a period of decades, a company must continually develop new products to either expand existing markets or enter new ones. Once again Dell is an excellent example because as the personal computer market has matured, the company has expanded its product offerings into computer servers, consumer electronics, and printers. It is important to note, however, that Dell expanded into related markets where it retained a low-cost manufacturing advantage. When a company expands into completely unrelated markets, the results can be lackluster. (Did you know that Coca-Cola once grew shrimp and Gillette explored for oil?)

3. How effective are the company's research-and-development efforts in relation to its size?

To develop new products, a company's research-and-development (R&D) effort must be both efficient and effective. As an investor, you should find companies that derive the greatest benefit from each dollar spent on R&D. For example, over the past 10 years, hard disk drive manufacturer Western Digital has earned over $27 billion in sales and spent about 5.8% of that, or $1.5 billion, on R&D. Yet during this time, Western Digital's cumulative operating loss totaled over $281 million. A much smaller semiconductor company, Linear Technology, had revenue of $5.6 billion over the past decade and spent a much larger percentage of it (11.5%, or $650 million) on R&D. Nonetheless, Linear earned cumulative operating income of $1.4 billion over this period.

When we compare the two companies, we see that Western Digital lost about $0.19 for each dollar spent on R&D, while Linear earned $2.13 for each R&D dollar. As you can see from the chart below, Linear has by a wide margin been the much more rewarding investment.

Linear Technology Versus Western Digital

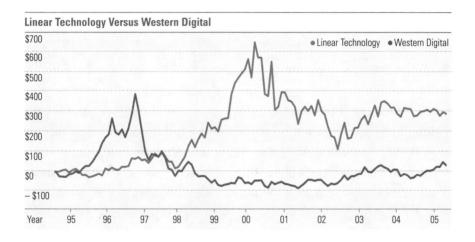

4. Does the company have an above-average sales organization?

Fisher wrote that in a competitive environment, few products or services are so compelling that they will sell to their maximum potential without expert merchandising. Therefore, an investor must carefully assess the relative effectiveness of a company's salesforce, advertising, and distribution.

5. Does the company have a worthwhile profit margin?

Berkshire Hathaway's vice-chairman Charlie Munger is fond of saying that if something is not worth doing, it is not worth doing well. Similarly, a company can show tremendous growth, but the growth must bring worthwhile profits to reward investors.

For instance, Western Digital's annual sales increased by 10% on average over the past 10 years, but that growth provided little in the way of profits since Western Digital's operating profit margins averaged negative 1.6%. On the other hand, Linear Technology grew at an impressive 17% average annual rate during the same period, while its operating margins averaged an astounding 51%. It's clear why investors in Linear Technology have fared much better than their counterparts in Western Digital.

6. What is the company doing to maintain or improve profit margins?

Linear Technology's record of the last 10 years may be stellar, but as Fisher stated, "It is not the profit margin of the past but those of the future that are basically important to the investor." Because inflation increases a company's expenses and competitors will pressure profit margins, you should pay attention to a company's strategy for reducing costs and improving profit margins over the long haul. This is where the moat framework we've spoken about throughout this workbook series can be a big help.

7. Does the company have outstanding labor and personnel relations?

According to Fisher, a company with good labor relations tends to be more profitable than one with mediocre relations because happy employees are likely to be more productive. There is no single yardstick to measure the state of a company's labor relations, but there are a few items investors should investigate.

First, companies with good labor relations usually make every effort to settle employee grievances quickly. In addition, a company that makes above-average profits, even while paying above-average wages to its employees is likely to have good labor relations. For example, Linear Technology clearly earns above-average profits and pays its rank and file employees as much as 40% of their base salary as a profit-sharing bonus.

Finally, investors should pay attention to the attitude of top management toward employees. If management does nothing to make employees feel wanted, then the company is unlikely to be an exceptionally desirable investment.

8. Does the company have outstanding executive relations?

Just as having good employee relations is important, a company must also cultivate the right atmosphere in its executive suite. Fisher noted that in companies where the founding family retains control, family members should not be promoted ahead of more able executives. In addition, executive salaries should be at least in line with industry norms. Salaries should also be reviewed regularly so that merited pay increases are given without having to be demanded.

9. Does the company have depth to its management?

As a company continues to grow over a span of decades, it is vital that a deep pool of management talent be properly developed. Fisher warned investors to avoid companies where top management is reluctant to delegate significant authority to lower-level managers. At some point, the company becomes too large for one or two executives to manage effectively, and without a deep bench of internally developed managers, the company will eventually encounter trouble.

This is a good example of an area where reading financial statements will not give you any insight. Rather, investigating the company via scuttlebutt comes in handy.

10. How good are the company's cost analysis and accounting controls?

A company cannot deliver outstanding results over the long term if it is unable to closely track costs in each step of its operations. Without this detailed information, a company cannot intelligently set prices or concentrate its sales efforts in specific areas. Fisher stated that getting a precise handle on a company's cost analysis is difficult, but an investor can discern which companies are exceptionally deficient—these are the companies to avoid.

11. Are there other aspects of the business, somewhat peculiar to the industry involved, which will give the investor important clues as to how outstanding the company may be in relation to its competition?

Fisher described this point as a catch-all because the "important clues" will vary widely among industries. The skill with which a retailer, like Wal-Mart or Costco, handles its merchandising and inventory is of paramount importance. However, in an industry such as insurance, a completely different set of business factors is important. It is critical for an investor to understand which industry factors determine the success of a company and how that company stacks up in relation to its rivals.

12. Does the company have a short-range or long-range outlook in regard to profits?

Fisher argued that investors should take a long-range view, and thus should favor companies that take a long-range view on profits. Companies that squeeze suppliers or customers for short-term profit will fail to build the goodwill that leads to greater overall profit over a span of many years. In addition, companies focused on meeting Wall Street's quarterly earnings estimates may forgo beneficial long-term actions if they cause a short-term hit to earnings. Even worse, management may be tempted to make aggressive accounting assumptions in order to report an acceptable quarterly profit number.

13. In the foreseeable future, will the growth of the company require sufficient equity financing so that the larger number of shares then outstanding will largely cancel the existing stockholders' benefit from this anticipated growth?

Imagine you owned a small slice of a growing pizza. As the pizza grows larger, you would expect that your piece of it should grow as well. However, if the pizza is constantly cut into ever smaller pieces, your slice may remain the same or become smaller even though the overall pizza is larger.

This is what happens when a company must continually issue new equity to fund its growth. For example, telecommunications firm Level 3 Communications has seen its sales more than triple since 2000, but its shares outstanding have increased from 363 million to 690 million (with another 172 million shares that could potentially be issued). Level 3 shareholders have seen their pizza slices shrink significantly. Shares of stock represent a partial ownership interest of a business. As an investor, you should seek companies with sufficient cash or borrowing capacity to fund growth without diluting the interests of its current owners.

14. Does management talk freely to investors about its affairs when things are going well but "clam up" when troubles and disappointments occur?

Every business, no matter how wonderful, will occasionally face disappointments. Investors should seek out management that reports candidly to shareholders all aspects of the business, good or bad. Warren Buffett is an exemplar in this area. His stated goal when reporting to Berkshire Hathaway shareholders is to provide all the information he would want if the positions were reversed. On the other hand, executives who refuse to talk about problems reveal that they may not have a plan in place to overcome the difficulties or have become panicky. In any case, Fisher's advice to avoid such management teams is sound.

15. Does the company have a management of unquestionable integrity?

The accounting scandals that led to the bankruptcies of Enron and World-Com should highlight the importance of investing only with management teams of unquestionable integrity. The corporate abuses that Fisher detailed, such as companies buying property from insiders at inflated prices or excessive stock option grants to executives, are still prevalent today. Investors will be well-served by following Fisher's warning that regardless of how highly a company rates on the other 14 points, "If there is a serious question of the lack of a strong management sense of trusteeship for shareholders, the investor should never seriously consider participating in such an enterprise."

Important Don'ts for Investors

In investing, the actions you don't take are as important as the actions you do take. Here is some of Fisher's advice on what you should not do.

1. Don't overstress diversification.

Investment advisors and the financial media constantly expound the virtues of diversification with the help of a catchy cliché: "Don't put all your eggs in one basket." However, as Fisher noted, once you start putting your eggs in a multitude of baskets, not all of them end up in attractive places, and it becomes difficult to keep track of all your eggs.

Fisher, who owned at most only 30 stocks at any point in his career, had a better solution. Spend time thoroughly researching and understanding a company, and if it clearly meets the 15 points he set forth, you should make a meaningful investment. Fisher would agree with Mark Twain when he said, "Put all your eggs in one basket, and watch that basket!"

2. Don't follow the crowd.

Following the crowds into investment fads, such as the "Nifty Fifty" in the early 1970s or tech stocks in the late 1990s, can be dangerous to your financial health. On the flip side, searching in areas the crowd has left behind can be extremely profitable. Sir Isaac Newton once lamented that he could calculate the motion of heavenly bodies, but not the madness of crowds. Fisher would heartily agree.

3. Don't quibble over eighths and quarters.

After extensive research, you've found a company that you think will prosper in the decades ahead, and the stock is currently selling at a reasonable price. Should you delay or forgo your investment to wait for a price a few pennies below the current price?

Fisher told the story of a skilled investor who wanted to purchase shares in a particular company whose stock closed that day at $35.50 per share. However, the investor refused to pay more than $35. The stock never again sold at $35 and over the next 25 years, increased in value to more than $500 per share. The investor missed out on a tremendous gain in a vain attempt to save 50 cents per share.

Even Warren Buffett is prone to this type of mental error. Buffett began purchasing Wal-Mart many years ago, but stopped buying when the price moved up a little. Buffett admits that this mistake cost Berkshire Hathaway shareholders about $10 billion. Even the Oracle of Omaha could have benefited from Fisher's advice not to quibble over eighths and quarters.

The Bottom Line

Philip Fisher compiled a sterling record during his seven-decade career by investing in young companies with bright growth prospects. By applying Fisher's methods, you, too, can uncover tomorrow's dominant companies.

Investor's Checklist

▶ Fisher's career spanned 74 years. After training as an analyst, Fisher started his San Francisco–based investment advisory firm in 1931. His classic book on investing, *Common Stocks and Uncommon Profits*, was first published in 1958.

▶ Fisher said that, "If the job has been correctly done when a common stock is purchased, the time to sell it is almost never." As an example, Fisher first purchased shares of Motorola in 1955 and held them until his death in 2004.

▶ Fisher put all of his potential investments through a 15-step checklist in order to gauge the quality of a company.

▶ According to Fisher, there are only three reasons to sell a stock: 1) If you have made a serious mistake in your assessment of the company; 2) If the company no longer passes the 15 points as clearly as before; 3) If you could reinvest the money in another, far more attractive company.

Quiz

1   Fisher was the author of which classic investment book?

a	*Security Analysis.*
b	*One Up on Wall Street.*
c	*Common Stocks and Uncommon Profits.*

Answers to this quiz can be found on page 178

2   What sorts of companies did Fisher favor?

a	Young growth companies.
b	Companies with large dividends.
c	Companies in mature industries.

3   Fisher's time horizon for holding a well-selected stock can best be described as what?

a	Very long-term.
b	Short-term.
c	Three to five years.

4   Which statement would Fisher most agree with?

a	"I don't want a lot of good investments; I want a few outstanding ones."
b	"It is important to own a well-diversified portfolio of over 50 stocks to reduce risk."
c	"Large capitalization companies in mature and steady industries are the best investments."

5   According to Fisher, which of the following is not a reason to sell a stock?

a	The price of the stock has gone up.
b	You made a serious mistake in your assessment of the company.
c	There is a far more attractive investment available.

Worksheet

Answers to this worksheet can be found on page 187

1   In your own words, summarize Fisher's investment philosophy in one sentence.

2   Based on Fisher's 15 points, should you invest in a company with $1 billion in sales and a 1% profit margin or a company with $500 million in sales and a 10% profit margin?

3   Given companies with the following characteristics, decide if Fisher would likely "Research Further" or "Avoid."

Company has a new product with the potential to reach $500 million in sales in five years:

☐ Research Further   ☐ Avoid

Company's research-and-development efforts have consistently failed to produce products with sizable sales and profit potential:

☐ Research Further   ☐ Avoid

Company has a sales organization that is recognized to be one of the best in the industry:

☐ Research Further   ☐ Avoid

Company's management is obsessed with meeting Wall Street's quarterly profit estimates:

☐ Research Further   ☐ Avoid

Company has grown 100% over the past three years, funded by issuing 50% more shares:

☐ Research Further   ☐ Avoid

Company's management is as equally candid about failures as it is about successes:

☐ Research Further   ☐ Avoid

Lesson 307: Great Companies at Reasonable Prices—Warren Buffett

"In our view, though, investment students need only two well-taught courses—How to Value a Business, and How to Think About Market Prices."—*Warren Buffett*

Warren Buffett is widely regarded as the world's most successful investor, and it is no mistake we have repeatedly echoed his wisdom throughout this workbook series. The book value of his company, Berkshire Hathaway, compounded at 21.9% per year between 1965 and 2004. That is more than double the 10.4% pretax return to the S&P 500 over the same period. According to Forbes, Buffett is the world's second-richest man with a net worth of about $44 billion at this writing. But he didn't stumble across a giant oil field, develop software, or inherit wealth. Rather, he built his fortune solely through astute investing. Aspiring investors, then, will certainly benefit by studying his methods. Fortunately, Buffett has been forthcoming.

In Berkshire's 1977 annual report, Buffett described the central principles of his investment strategy:

"We select our marketable equity securities in much the way we would evaluate a business for acquisition in its entirety. We want the business to be one (a) that we can understand; (b) with favorable long-term prospects; (c) operated by honest and competent people; and (d) available at a very attractive price."

Determining Fair Value

Buffett determines the attractiveness of a company's price by comparing it with his estimate of the company's value. To determine value, he estimates the company's future cash flows and discounts them at an appropriate rate. Discounting is necessary because $1,000 today is worth more than $1,000 received after one year. If an investor can earn 6% interest on his or her money, then $1,000 today is worth $1,060 in one year. Conversely, an expected $1,000 cash flow one year from now is worth only $943.40 today, because $943.40 earning 6% grows to $1,000 in one year. (For more on discounted cash flow and the time value of money, see Lesson 211 in Workbook #2.)

This discounted cash-flow valuation method was described by John Burr Williams in his 1938 book, *The Theory of Investment Value*. It is used by countless investment professionals, so Buffett's approach to valuation is not a competitive advantage. However, his ability to estimate future cash flows more accurately than other investors is an advantage.

Another part of his edge may be due to his sharp mind, but Buffett insists that successful investing doesn't require a high IQ; it depends more on a successful framework and having the proper temperament. Buffett succeeds largely because he focuses his efforts on companies with durable competitive advantages that fall within his circle of competence. These are key features of his investing framework.

Understanding Your Circle of Competence

If Buffett cannot understand a company's business, then it lies beyond his circle of competence, and he won't attempt to value it. He famously avoided technology stocks in the late 1990s in part because he had no expertise in technology. On the other hand, Buffett continued to buy and hold what he knew. For instance, he was willing to purchase a large stake in Coca-Cola because he understood the company's products and its business model.

Although it might seem obvious that investors should stick to what they know, the temptation to step outside one's circle of competence can be strong. During the technology stock mania of 1999, Berkshire's return badly trailed the market's return, and a number of observers commented that Buffett was hopelessly behind the times for eschewing technology stocks.

However, Buffett has written that he isn't bothered when he misses out on big returns in areas he doesn't understand, because investors can do very well (as he has) by simply avoiding big mistakes. He believes that what counts most for investors is not so much what they know but how realistically they can define what they don't know.

Buying Companies with Sustainable Competitive Advantages

Even if a business is easy to understand, Buffett won't attempt to value it if its future cash flows are unpredictable. He wants to own simple, stable businesses that possess sustainable competitive advantages. Companies with these characteristics are highly likely to generate materially higher cash flows with the passage of time. Without these characteristics, valuation estimates become very uncertain.

His large stake in Coca-Cola provides us with an example of the type of company he favors. Coca-Cola is more than 100 years old, and it has been selling essentially the same product during its entire existence. Coke was the leading soft drink in 1896 just as it is today. It seems unlikely that customers will ever lose their taste for it. Buffett believes that the product and the Coca-Cola brand are durable competitive advantages that will enable the company to earn economic profits for shareholders for many years to come.

On the other hand, technology is a fast-changing industry where the leading company of today can be driven out of business tomorrow by more innovative rivals. Market-leading products are always vulnerable to obsolescence. Thus, even if Buffett had technological expertise, he would be reluctant to invest in the industry because he couldn't be confident that a technology company's cash flows would be materially higher in 10 or 20 years, or even that the company would still exist.

Buffett's Investments

Buffett's investing style is made plain by the types of companies his holding company, Berkshire Hathaway, has either invested in or bought outright.

Prominent Wholly Owned Companies

Company	Main Business	Company	Main Business
Gen Re	Insurance	Helzberg Diamonds	Jewelry
GEICO	Insurance	FlightSafety International	Pilot Training
MidAmerican Holdings	Pipelines & Utilities	McLane	Trucking
NetJets	Corporate Jet Rental	Fruit of the Loom	Garments
Shaw Carpets	Carpets	Benjamin Moore	Paint
Clayton Homes	Manufactured Housing	Dairy Queen	Ice-cream Franchising

10 Largest Common Stock Investments

American Express	Washington Post
Coca-Cola	PetroChina
Gillette	White Mountains Insurance
Wells Fargo	M&T Bank
Moody's	H&R Block

As of Dec. 31, 2004

Partnering with Admirable Managers

Buffett seeks businesses with talented, likeable managers already in place. Although he has the ability to change the management at Berkshire's wholly owned subsidiaries, Buffett believes that power is "somewhat illusory" because "management changes, like marital changes, are painful, time-consuming, and chancy." He has written that good managers are unlikely to triumph over a bad business, but given a business with decent economic characteristics—the only type that interests him—good managers make a significant difference. He looks for individuals who are more passionate about their work than their compensation and who exhibit energy, intelligence, and integrity. That last quality is especially important to him. He believes that he has never made a good deal with a bad person.

Omaha native and Berkshire Hathaway vice chairman Charlie Munger has been Warren Buffett's friend and alter ego for more than 40 years. Buffett confers with Munger regularly and credits him with improving Buffett's investment decision-making. In particular, Munger has encouraged Buffett to purchase superior businesses even if they are not available at deep discounts to their economic value. This is a departure from Ben Graham's approach of seeking bargain prices with little regard for the quality of the business. Read ahead to Lesson 309 for more on Munger.

Charlie Munger

An Approach to Market Prices

Once Buffett has decided that he is competent to evaluate a company, that the company has sustainable advantages, and that it is run by commendable managers, then he still has to decide whether or not to buy it. This step is the most crucial part of the process so it deserves the most attention.

The decision process seems simple enough: If the market price is below the discounted cash-flow calculation of fair value, then the security is a candidate for purchase. The available securities that offer the greatest discounts to fair value estimates are the ones to buy.

However, what seems simple in theory is difficult in practice. A company's stock price typically drops when investors shun it because of bad news, so a buyer of cheap securities is constantly swimming against the tide of popular sentiment. Even investments that generate excellent long-term returns can perform poorly for years. In fact, Buffett wrote an article in 1979 explaining that stocks were undervalued, yet the undervaluation only worsened for another three years. Most investors find it difficult to buy when it seems that everyone is selling, and difficult to remain steadfast when returns are poor for several consecutive years.

Buffett credits his late friend and mentor, Benjamin Graham, with teaching him the appropriate attitude toward market prices. You may remember Graham's parable in which he said to imagine daily quotations as coming from Mr. Market, your very temperamental partner in a private business.

Each day he offers you a price for which he will buy your share of the business, or for which you can buy his share of the business. On some days he is euphoric and offers you a very high price for your share. On other days he is despondent and offers a very low price. Mr. Market doesn't mind if you abuse or ignore him—he'll be back with another price tomorrow.

The most important thing to remember about Mr. Market is that he offers you the potential to make a profit, but he does not offer useful guidance. If an investor can't evaluate his business better than Mr. Market, then the investor doesn't belong in that business. Thus, Buffett invests only in predictable businesses that he understands, and he ignores the judgment of Mr. Market (the daily market price) except to take advantage of Mr. Market's mistakes.

Requiring a Margin of Safety

Although Buffett believes the market is frequently wrong about the fair value of stocks, he doesn't believe himself to be infallible. If he estimates a company's fair value at $80 per share, and the company's stock sells for $77, he will refrain from buying despite the apparent undervaluation. That small discrepancy does not provide an adequate margin of safety, another concept borrowed from Ben Graham. No one can predict cash flows into the distant future with precision, not even for stable businesses with durable competitive advantages. Therefore, any estimate of fair value must include substantial room for error.

For instance, if a stock's estimated value is $80 per share, then a purchase at $60 allows an investor to be wrong by 25% but still achieve a satisfactory result. The $20 difference between estimated fair value and purchase price is what Graham called the margin of safety. Buffett considers this margin-of-safety principle to be the cornerstone of investment success.

Concentrating on Your Best Ideas

Buffett has difficulty finding understandable businesses with sustainable competitive advantages and excellent managers that also sell at discounts to their estimated fair values. Therefore, his investment portfolio has often been concentrated in relatively few companies. This practice is at odds with the Modern Portfolio Theory taught in business schools, but Buffett rejects the idea that diversification is helpful to informed investors. On the contrary, he thinks the addition of an investor's 20th favorite holding is likely to lower returns and increase risk compared with simply adding the same amount of money to the investor's top choices.

Every publicly traded corporation has annual shareholder meetings, but most are poorly attended affairs held primarily to satisfy a regulatory requirement. On the other hand, Berkshire Hathaway's meetings resemble an annual pilgrimage of devoted shareholders who come to hear the wit and wisdom of Warren Buffett and Charlie Munger. The yearly gatherings, which now draw an estimated 20,000 attendees, have been described as the "Woodstock of Capitalism."

The Pilgrimage to Omaha

The Bottom Line

Buffett's thinking permeates Morningstar's philosophy and valuation framework. We fully believe that you can greatly boost your investment returns if you invest like Buffett. This means staying within your circle of competence, focusing on companies with wide economic moats, paying attention to company valuation and not market prices, and finally requiring a margin of safety before buying.

Investor's Checklist

▶ Buffett uses a discounted cash-flow analysis to estimate the fair value of companies.

▶ Unless analyzing a business falls within his circle of competence, Buffett does not try to value the business.

▶ Buffett seeks companies with sustainable competitive advantages. (Companies with economic moats.)

▶ Though Buffett believes it's important to work with competent, honest managers, the economics of a business are the most important factor.

▶ Buffett is not swayed by popular opinion.

▶ Since no discounted cash-flow analysis is perfect, Buffett requires a margin of safety in his purchase price.

▶ Rather than diversify and dilute his potential returns, Buffett concentrates his investments on his best ideas.

Quiz

1   Buffett believes that portfolio diversification:

Answers to this quiz can be found on page 178

a	Reduces risk because it lessens the impact of any single bad investment.
b	Probably increases risk for informed investors by diluting the effect of their top choices, the companies with the least risk and highest potential returns.
c	Is an important part of his investment framework.

2   Buffett avoids technology stocks for all of the following reasons except:

a	He has no technological expertise.
b	Although they offer the highest returns, technology stocks are too volatile.
c	The technology industry changes rapidly so it is too difficult to determine which competitive advantages, if any, might be sustainable.

3   A margin of safety is:

a	The difference between a company's estimated fair value and its stock price (where the price is lower than the fair value).
b	Provided by portfolio diversification.
c	Unnecessary for skilled, informed investors like Buffett.

4   All of the following statements are false except:

a	Good managers are likely to succeed even if they run a business with poor economic characteristics.
b	Because Buffett has the power to change the management of his wholly owned subsidiaries, he doesn't worry about the managers in place at the time of purchase.
c	Buffett believes that he has never made a good deal with bad people.

5   All of the following statements are false except:

a	Buffett believes that stock market prices are sometimes much too high or too low.
b	Buffett frequently uses stop-loss orders to cap his risk.
c	Buffett prefers to buy stocks after they have "broken-out" to new highs.

Worksheet

Answers to this worksheet can
be found on page 188

1   Say you perform a discounted cash-flow analysis to arrive at Company Z's estimated fair value of $50 per share. The stock price is currently $40 per share. If you purchase Company Z now, what is your margin of safety?

2   You have determined that the stock of Company Y is worth $20 per share, and you are able to purchase it for only $15 per share. However, after purchase, the stock price plunges to $10 per share. Should you sell the stock to avoid greater losses?

3   Visit the home page of Berkshire Hathaway (www.berkshirehathaway.com) or obtain the most recent annual report for the company. These are treasure troves of investing wisdom worth digging into. After reading one of these, would you describe Buffett's style as simple or flashy?

Lesson 308: Know What You Own—Peter Lynch

"Gig my gigahertz and whetstone my megaflop, if you couldn't tell if that was a racehorse or a memory chip you should stay away from it."—Peter Lynch

Peter Lynch is one of the greatest money managers and most famous investors of all time. He drew acclaim for his success as the portfolio manager of Fidelity Magellan, the mutual fund he ran from 1977 to 1990. When Lynch became Magellan's manager in 1977, the fund had $20 million in assets. Lynch's strong track record at Magellan drew investors at a rapid rate, and by 1983 the fund's assets topped $1 billion. During the 13 years Lynch ran the fund, Magellan outperformed the annual return of the S&P 500 stock index 11 years. Lynch achieved this performance even after Magellan was the nation's largest mutual fund with $13 billion in assets. The sheer size of Magellan was part of Lynch's aura. No one else had managed such a big fund with so much success.

Despite his uncanny talent as a portfolio manager, Lynch's mantra is that average investors have an edge over Wall Street experts. He says that professional investors usually don't find a stock genuinely attractive until a number of large institutions have recognized its suitability and an equal number of respected Wall Street analysts have put it on the recommended list. This "Street lag" gives average investors many advantages because they can find promising investments largely ahead of the professional investors. Lynch stated, "If you stay half-alert, you can pick the spectacular performers right from your place of business or out of the neighborhood shopping mall, and long before Wall Street discovers them." Therefore, individual investors can outperform the experts and the market in general by looking around for investment ideas in their everyday lives.

Lynch's seminal book, *One Up on Wall Street*, articulates his investment philosophy. The Lynch stock-picking approach has several key principles: First, you should invest only in what you understand. Second, you should do your homework and research an investment thoroughly. Third, you should focus more on a company's fundamentals and not the market as a whole. Last, you should invest only for the long run and discard short-term market gyrations. If you adhere to the basic principles of this investment philosophy, Lynch believes that you will be well on your way to "beating the street."

Stick to What You Know

Investing in what you know about and understand is at the core of Lynch's stock-picking approach. This particular investment principle served Lynch very well in practice. Lynch invested only in industries he had a firm grasp on, such as the auto industry. That's what led him to Chrysler (today part of DaimlerChrysler) back in the early 1980s. Chrysler was getting beat up by the competition and was near bankruptcy—it seemed the carmaker would never regain its footing. But after seeing prototypes of a new thing called a minivan, Lynch made Chrysler one of Magellan's top holdings. It paid off, and Chrysler more than tripled in price while Magellan owned it.

Moreover, Lynch has pointed out that you will find your best investment ideas close to home. He claimed, "An amateur investor can pick tomorrow's big winners by paying attention to new developments at the workplace, the mall, the auto showrooms, the restaurants, or anywhere a promising new enterprise makes its debut." For example, Lynch said that after his wife raved over the fact that Hanes Co. (now owned by Sara Lee) conveniently sold its L'eggs pantyhose in grocery stores, he figured the company was on to something good. His hunch was right. Hanes' stock rose sixfold while Magellan held it. Lynch's main point here is to look around you because that's where you are most likely to find your winners.

Things Lynch Looks For, and Avoids

Company Characteristics that Might Attract Lynch:

▶ It is boring.

▶ The industry is not growing.

▶ The business is specialized and entrenched.

▶ The business sounds silly.

▶ There is a lot of controversy surrounding the business.

▶ It has been spun out of a larger company.

▶ Wall Street doesn't follow it or care about it.

▶ The business supplies something people need to continually buy.

▶ Management is buying shares, or the company is repurchasing its stock.

▶ It uses technology to cut costs or add value for customers.

Company Characteristics that Might Repel Lynch:

▶ Company or its industry is grabbing a lot of headlines.

▶ It is the hot topic of conversation at happy hour.

▶ It is being touted as a revolutionary company that is the next great investment.

▶ It has a cool, futuristic name.

▶ It is diversifying too much, diluting its competitive strengths.

▶ It is a middleman and has a limited number of clients.

Do Your Research and Set Reasonable Expectations

The second key principle in Lynch's investment philosophy is that you should do your homework and research the company thoroughly. Lynch remarked, "Investing without research is like playing stud poker and never looking at the cards." He recommends reading all prospectuses, quarterly reports (Form 10-Q), and annual reports (Form 10-K) that companies are required to file with the Securities and Exchange Commission. If any pertinent information is unavailable in the annual report, Lynch says that you will be able to find it by asking your broker, calling the company, visiting the company, or doing some grassroots research, also known as "kicking the tires." After completing the research process, you should be familiar with the company's business and have developed some sense of its future potential.

Once you have done your research on a company, Lynch believes that it is important to set some realistic expectations about each stock's potential. He usually ranks the companies by size and then places them into one of six categories: slow growers, stalwarts, fast growers, cyclicals, turnarounds, and asset plays.

Slow Growers. Large and aging companies that are expected to grow slightly faster than the gross national product but generally pay a large and regular dividend. Lynch doesn't invest much in slow growers because companies that aren't growing fast will not see rapid appreciation in their stock price.

Stalwarts. Large companies that grow at a faster rate than slow growers, with annual earnings growth rates of about 10%-12%. Lynch believes that stalwarts offer sizable profits when you buy them cheap, but he doesn't expect to make more than a 30%-50% return on them.

Fast Growers. Small, aggressive, new companies that grow at 20%-25% a year. These companies don't have to be in fast-growing industries per se, and Lynch favors those that are not. Lynch thinks that fast growers are the big winners in the stock market, but they also have a considerable amount of risk.

Cyclicals. Companies whose sales and profits rise and fall in a regular fashion. Lynch states that cyclicals are the most misunderstood stocks, and they are often confused for stalwarts by inexperienced investors. Investing in cyclicals requires a keen sense of timing and the ability to detect the early signs in a cycle.

Turnarounds. Companies that have been battered and depressed, and are often close to bankruptcy. Lynch notes that such "no growers" can make up lost ground very quickly, and their upswings are generally tied to the overall market.

Asset Plays. Companies with valuable assets that Wall Street analysts have missed. While Lynch says that asset opportunities are everywhere, he points out that you will need a working knowledge of the company and a healthy dose of patience.

Know the Fundamentals

The third main principle of Lynch's stock-picking approach is to focus only on the company's fundamentals and not the market as a whole. Lynch doesn't believe in predicting markets, but he believes in buying great companies—especially companies that are undervalued and/or underappreciated. One might say Lynch advocates looking at companies one at a time using a "bottom up" approach rather trying to make difficult macroeconomic calls using a "top down" approach.

While he generally looks for great businesses trading at bargain prices, Lynch underscores the importance of strong earnings growth—a measure of profitability. Lynch has said, "People may bet on the hourly wiggles in the market, but it's the earnings that waggle the wiggles, long-term." Although he doesn't think average investors can predict actual growth rates, Lynch suggests that you should consider how a company plans to boost its earnings. He has outlined five basic ways a company can increase its earnings: reduce costs; raise prices; expand into new markets; sell more of its product in old markets; or revitalize, close, or dispose of a losing operation. By analyzing how a company will grow its earnings, Lynch believes that you should be able to determine a stock's potential.

The Importance of Earnings Growth

Lynch believes that investors can separate good companies from mediocre ones by sticking to the fundamentals and combing through financial statements. He suggests looking at some of the following famous numbers, which happen to be many of the same numbers that stock analysts at Morningstar look for.

Percent of Sales. If your interest in a company stems from a specific product, be sure to find out if it represents a meaningful percent of sales. It doesn't make sense to remain interested if this number is inconsequential.

Year-Over-Year Earnings. Look for stability and consistency in year-over-year earnings. In the long run, a stock's earnings and price will move in tandem, so look for companies with earnings that consistently go up.

Earnings Growth. Make sure a company's earnings growth reflects its true prospects. High levels of earnings growth are rarely sustainable, but high growth could be factored into a stock's price.

The P/E Ratio (Lynch's favorite metric). Think of the P/E ratio as the number of years it will take the company to earn back your initial investment (assuming constant earnings). Keep in mind that slow growers will have low P/E ratios and fast growers high ones. It is particularly useful to look at a company's P/E ratio relative to its earnings growth rate (PEG ratio). Generally speaking, a P/E ratio that's half the growth rate is very attractive, and one that's twice the growth rate is very unattractive. Avoid excessively high P/E ratios and remember that P/E ratios are not comparable across industries. However, comparing a company's current P/E ratio with benchmarks such as its historical P/E average, industry P/E average, and the market's P/E can help you determine if the stock is cheap, fully valued, or overpriced.

The Cash Position. Look for a company's cash position on the balance sheet. A strong cash position affords a company financial stability and can represent a built-in discount for investors in the stock.

The Debt Factor. Check to see if the company has significant long-term debt on its balance sheet. If it does, this could be a considerable disadvantage when business is good (can't grow) or bad (can't pay the interest expense).

Dividends. If you are interested in dividend-paying firms, look for those that have the ability to pay out dividends during recessions and a long track record of regularly raising dividends.

Book Value. Remember that the stated book value often bears little relationship to the actual worth of the company because it often understates or overstates reality by a large margin.

Cash Flow. Always look for companies that throw off lots of free cash flow, which is the cash that's left over after normal capital spending.

Inventories. Make sure that inventories are growing in line with sales. If inventories are piling up and sales stagnating, this could be an important red flag. Inventories are particularly important numbers for cyclical firms.

Pension Plans. If a company has a pension plan, make sure that plan assets exceed vested benefit liabilities.

Ignoring Mr. Market

The last key principle of Lynch's investment philosophy is that you should only invest for the long run and discard short-term market gyrations. Lynch has said, "Absent a lot of surprises, stocks are relatively predictable over ten to twenty years. As to whether they're going to be higher or lower in two or three years, you might as well flip a coin to decide." It might seem surprising to hear Lynch make this argument, because portfolio managers are typically evaluated based on short-term performance metrics. Nonetheless, Lynch sticks with his philosophy, adding: "When it comes to the market, the important skill here is not listening, it's snoring. The trick is not to learn to trust your gut feelings, but rather to discipline yourself to ignore them. Stand by your stocks as long as the fundamental story has not changed."

Comparing Lynch and Buffett	Lynch's investment philosophy is very similar to Buffett's stock-picking approach, which Morningstar also emulates. Lynch said, "And Warren Buffett, the greatest investor of them all, looks for the same opportunities I do, except that when he finds them [great businesses at bargain prices], he buys the whole company."

The Bottom Line

Lynch firmly believes that average investors can beat Wall Street professionals. He recommends investing only in what you understand and doing your research. By finding great companies with strong fundamentals at bargain prices, he argues that you will have the next big winners in hand before the professional investors. Lynch encapsulated this point well when he said, "The basic story remains simple and never-ending. Stocks aren't lottery tickets. There's a company attached to every share. Companies do better or they do worse. If a company does worse than before, its stock will fall. If a company does better, its stock will rise. If you own good companies that continue to increase their earnings, you'll do well."

Investor's Checklist

▶ Lynch obtained his legendary investor status managing the Fidelity Magellan Fund. Under Lynch's leadership, the Magellan fund grew from $20 million in assets to $13 billion and achieved an average total return of 25% per year.

▶ Despite his success as a professional money manager, Lynch believes that average investors have an edge over Wall Street experts and can outperform the market by looking for investment ideas in their daily lives.

▶ The Lynch investment philosophy has four main components:
1. Invest only in what you understand.
2. Do your homework and research the company thoroughly.
3. Focus only on the company's fundamentals and not the market as a whole.
4. Invest only for the long run and discard short-term market gyrations.

▶ Although he is best known for trend-spotting, Lynch's stock-picking approach mirrors that of Warren Buffett.

Quiz

Answers to this quiz can be found on page 179

1   Lynch's track record with which fund helped build his name?

a	Fidelity Megan Fund.
b	Fidelity Magellan Fund.
c	Fidelity Contrafund.

2   What sorts of companies did Lynch favor?

a	Those in hot industries.
b	Those in industries he understood.
c	Those in esoteric industries.

3   Lynch's investment style is best described as what?

a	Value.
b	Growth.
c	Opportunistic.

4   What three fundamental criteria did Lynch use to evaluate a stock?

a	Profits, business model, and current stock price.
b	Profits, price/earnings ratio, and valuation model.
c	Profits, debt, and current stock price.

5   Which was not a part of Lynch's stock-picking approach?

a	Invest in what you know.
b	Invest for the long run.
c	Focus on the market and the short term.

Worksheet

Answers to this worksheet can be found on page 189

1   Lynch claims that the best investment ideas are found close to home. Look for new developments at your workplace, mall, auto showrooms, restaurants, or anywhere a promising new enterprise makes its debut. What are some of your promising candidates?

2   What are the four key principles of Lynch's investment philosophy?

1.

2.

3.

4.

3   Based on Lynch's stock-picking approach, should you invest in doughnuts or semiconductors?

continued…

109

Worksheet

Answers to this worksheet can be found on page 189

4   Given companies with the following characteristics, decide if Lynch would likely "Research Further" or "Avoid."

Company has pension liabilities that far exceed its pension assets:

☐ Research Further   ☐ Avoid

Company has earnings growth rate that is triple its P/E ratio:

☐ Research Further   ☐ Avoid

Company's insiders are buying the stock:

☐ Research Further   ☐ Avoid

Company is in a fast-growth industry Lynch knows little about:

☐ Research Further   ☐ Avoid

Company is on the cover of several large magazines:

☐ Research Further   ☐ Avoid

Company spends a lot of money every year on acquisitions in various industries:

☐ Research Further   ☐ Avoid

Company is touted on television as "the next Microsoft":

☐ Research Further   ☐ Avoid

Company creates simple, widely recognized but low-growth product:

☐ Research Further   ☐ Avoid

Lesson 309: The Rest of the Hall of Fame

"The characteristic of genuine heroism is its persistency. All men have wandering impulses, fits and starts of generosity. But when you have resolved to be great, abide by yourself, and do not weakly try to reconcile yourself with the world. The heroic cannot be the common, nor the common the heroic."—*Ralph Waldo Emerson*

Most successful investors take a few ideas from several others and spin those ideas into their own. In the previous lessons, we've highlighted some of the greatest investors of our era, however there are certainly many more. In this lesson, we'll introduce you to a few more money managers we think deserve a spot in the "Investing Hall of Fame." Make sure to look for the common investing themes across these superb stock-pickers.

Charlie Munger—Investing with Worldly Wisdom

Charlie Munger, vice chairman of Berkshire Hathaway, is often overshadowed by his colleague Warren Buffett. However, much of the investment philosophy employed by Buffett and Berkshire can be attributed to Munger's influence.

Like Buffett, Munger is from Nebraska. He started his career as a lawyer, but through his friendship with Buffett, Munger eventually left his successful law career to join Buffett in running Berkshire Hathaway. Over the years, the two have developed a great rapport, often highlighted during Berkshire Hathaway's annual meetings. When shareholders pepper the two with queries during question-and-answer sessions, Buffett will give his usual insightful thoughts, while Munger answers with his dry witty remarks, often leaving listeners in stitches.

Here's one gem from the 2005 shareholder meeting, where Buffett and Munger discussed the compensation committees of many boards of directors:

Buffett: I've been on 19 boards, and I've never seen a director to whom fees were important object to an acquisition or a CEO's compensation—members of compensation committees act like Chihuahuas, not Great Danes or Dobermans. [Pause] I hope I'm not insulting any of my friends who are on compensation committees.

Munger: You're insulting the dogs.

Munger helped Buffett develop his knack for not only finding undervalued stocks, but for investing in strong businesses with strong competitive advantages. In other words, business quality truly matters to Munger, not just how cheap a stock is.

Munger also urges investors to gain worldly wisdom to become successful at stock-picking. This means that investors should not just focus on a few narrow topics but expand their horizons to understand many different subjects. For example, an engineer should learn accounting to understand how a business can make a profit. Likewise, a good financial analyst shouldn't just crunch numbers but also learn how the machines in a factory work. This worldly wisdom helps investors gain knowledge about the way things work in a broad sense, which in turn helps them to better understand the economics of a certain business. With worldly wisdom, investors can stay focused on what matters while others are running for the doors due to a short-term blip. In other words, the worldly wisdom Munger preaches can help savvy investors profit from others' shortsightedness.

Wesco Financial
Charlie Munger is also chairman of Wesco Financial, which is 80% owned by Berkshire Hathaway. The strategy at Wesco is similar to Berkshire's: Munger simply seeks to increase the company's intrinsic value per share and is agnostic about how this occurs. He scours the investment universe for companies he can purchase at attractive prices and will hold cash if no bargains are available.

Bill Miller—Value Outside the Box

Few investors have melded the growth and value schools of investing better than Bill Miller, manager of the Legg Mason Value Trust mutual fund. Some value-investing enthusiasts disagree that Miller is one of their own. While his practice of valuing stocks on the underlying businesses is acceptable, Miller has made some questionable "value" plays. Some famous examples include America Online, Dell Computer, and Amazon.com. Though none were of the traditional "value" mold, all these stocks made substantial price gains after Miller bought them.

Critics characterize Miller as a growth investor in a value investor's clothing, but a look into his thought processes reveals Miller's knack for seeing value where others don't. This ability has allowed the Legg Mason Value Fund to beat the s&p 500 for 14 consecutive years—a remarkable feat.

Like any value investor, Miller looks for businesses with strong competitive advantages that are trading below his estimates of the firms' worth. He uses a discounted cash-flow model to determine intrinsic value. Unlike many value managers, however, Miller is willing to make fairly optimistic assumptions about growth, and he doesn't shy away from owning companies in traditional growth sectors. In his fund, pricey Internet stocks rub elbows with bargain-priced financials and turnaround plays. Miller will also let favored names run, allowing top positions to soak up a large percentage of assets. This portfolio concentration may fly in the face of modern portfolio theory, but Miller isn't one to accept the conventional wisdom.

A more recent example of Miller's value/growth mix is his purchase of Google, a rapidly growing Internet search engine. While many investors shied away from this stock due to valuation concerns, Miller scooped up shares during its ipo. The stock doubled quickly after the company went public. While it's still too early to tell where Google will be 5 or 10 years down the road, this purchase was done in classic Bill Miller fashion—investing in a wildly profitable company that few investors understand or appreciate.

Bill Miller is also associated with the Santa Fe Institute, a New Mexico–based think-tank that works on understanding complex adaptive systems. Learning about these systems has helped Miller understand the way businesses will look several years down the road. Also, understanding human behavior, essentially what a complex adaptive system is, helps keep a clear head during irrational times.

Marty Whitman—Value in the Unloved

Marty Whitman is a vulture of a value investor. Whitman, manager of the Third Avenue Value Fund, can usually be found rummaging through the rubble of distressed stocks—those of beaten-down companies, some on the brink of insolvency. But most of Whitman's depressed stock plays eventually turn around for the better. The key to Whitmanesque stock-picking: Buy companies that are cheap (presumably because of some temporary issue) and safe, and hold on to them.

Whitman is a value investor after Benjamin Graham's own heart. Like Graham, Whitman looks for stocks that are dirt cheap, but the two investors use different measuring sticks. Graham used a company's price/book ratio to determine whether its stock was cheap. He generally wouldn't buy a company unless its stock was trading for less than 1.2 times book value per share.

Whitman takes a different approach. He focuses on a company's takeover value, or how much he thinks a buyer would pay to buy the whole company. Whitman doesn't like to use book value because he says it overlooks too many intangibles. For instance, a money-management firm can use its reputation and relationships to gain additional business. Its reputation and relationships are assets, so to speak, but they don't appear as such on a company's balance sheet. According to Whitman, takeover value accounts for such intangibles.

Whitman combs through a company's financial statements to figure out what he thinks the business is worth. He then checks to see whether the company's balance sheet has remained strong in spite of setbacks in the business. He will generally pay no more than 50% of what he thinks a buyer would pay to acquire the whole firm.

It can take a long time to unlock the value of a beaten-up stock. As long as a company is safe and cheap, Whitman is willing to wait.

Bill Nygren—Ignoring the Noise

Bill Nygren is the manager of the Oakmark Select mutual fund. He joined Harris Associates, advisor to the Oakmark funds, in 1983. After a stint as director of research for Harris Associates for most of the 1990s, Nygren began managing the Select fund in early 2000, near the height of the technology bubble. Value investing is always tough, but even tougher when a bubble exists in stock prices. During these times, the undervalued stocks usually stay cheap for a long time, while the expensive "hot stocks" of the moment keep going up. When Nygren took over, Oakmark's investors were jumping ship trying to take advantage of ever-increasing Internet and other technology stocks. By sticking to his guns, however, Nygren eventually proved that his methodology of buying growing, but undervalued, firms pays off in the long run.

Nygren buys stocks that are trading at discounts to their estimated private market values. To estimate a company's intrinsic value, Nygren and his colleagues use discounted cash-flow analysis and look at comparable transactions, among many other factors. When picking stocks, Nygren likes to look for companies he believes the market underappreciates, perhaps because of a short-term difficulty.

In a speech given in early 2005, Nygren described his investing philosophy using a variation of the 80/20 rule, a strategy made famous by his former portfolio holding, Illinois Tool Works. Nygren said he looks for stocks where 80% of the commentary about a company revolves around a piece of business that contributes only about 20% of the profits. When he finds a situation like this, it is likely the market is undervaluing the firm.

Such is the case with Nygren's largest holding (at the time of this writing), Washington Mutual. Much of the news about WaMu is about the company's troubled mortgage business, while most of the firm's profits come from the highly profitable and growing retail banking business. Nygren believes that once the market realizes its misplaced focus, WaMu's stock should appreciate. Only time will tell if Nygren is correct, but as a long-term buy-and-hold investor, Nygren can wait.

Stewardship Matters

Nygren also looks for companies that have management's interests truly aligned with those of shareholders. It is more likely that these firms will create value over time when the executives act like owners rather than employees.

Ralph Wanger—Success in Small Stocks

Ralph Wanger, semi-retired manager of Columbia Acorn Fund, searches for smaller stocks he believes have yet to be uncovered by Wall Street. Before investing in a company, Wanger looks for companies that are financially strong and have significant growth opportunities ahead of them. These are obvious criteria that most investors look for. However, while many small-cap growth investors are willing to overlook valuation for the upside potential of a stock, Wanger believes that growth should only be purchased at a reasonable price.

Markets often overvalue growth stocks, so this is an important point. On the plus side, however, the small companies Wanger looks for have often largely been ignored by the Wall Street analysts, thus many investors are not aware of potential opportunities. Since fewer investors are paying attention to smaller companies, the chance of finding an undervalued stock is more likely.

Rather than employ a top-down approach to investing, where investors first analyze macroeconomic trends such as GDP growth in a certain country, Wanger employs the ideas of investing according to themes. For example, if Wanger believes the population in China is becoming increasingly wealthy, he may look for consumer-goods makers that sell high-end items in the country.

Wanger isn't afraid to go against the trend either. In the late 1990s, many of his small-growth peers posted huge returns by betting that already high stock prices would be carried higher still by a wave of investor enthusiasm for technology stocks. (This is the so-called "greater fool" strategy.) That tactic, of course, was laden with risk, and many funds paid a huge price.

Amid it all, Wanger did what he always has: He sought out sound businesses with strong earnings and cash flows that appeared cheap. That tactic held Wanger's fund back in 1999, but he was eventually proven correct. From March 2000 through April 30, 2001, the fund gained 16.8% on a cumulative basis, while his typical small-growth peer lost a cumulative 31%. However, Wanger isn't in our Hall of Fame just for a few years of performance. A $10,000 investment in the fund in June 1970 would have grown to just less than $1.3 million if held through May 2003, around the time he stepped down from day-to-day duties. In contrast, the same money invested in the S&P 500 Index would have grown to just more than $400,000.

Bill Ruane—Value Investing at Its Best

Bill Ruane keeps his head when most others lose theirs. Ruane has been managing the Sequoia Fund since 1970, and with great success. A $10,000 investment in the fund back in 1970 would have been worth $1.7 million at the end of 2004. At many times, Ruane's investing strategy mirrors Warren Buffett's, and not by coincidence. Both of these great investors studied under Ben Graham at Columbia University, and even worked for him for a while. That's why such terms as "intrinsic value" and "margin of safety" often show up in Ruane's vocabulary. Given this, it's clear to see why, at the time of this writing, Berkshire Hathaway was the largest holding in Ruane's Sequoia Fund.

More Insightful Letters Ruane is also known for his insightful shareholder letters, where he spells out his thought processes and expresses opinions on various topics, such as mismanagement at mutual fund firms or technology bubbles. You can check out these letters, as well as the transcripts to his annual meetings, at the firm's Web site: www.sequoiafund.com.

Ruane looks for companies with sound finances and strong franchises, buying only the few whose stocks trade below their intrinsic values. Further, Ruane isn't afraid to buck traditional money management trends when necessary. For example, while many managers may scramble to chase hot stocks to fend off underperformance, Ruane's fund often sits on a pile of cash when he believes stock prices are too high. This strategy has certainly served shareholders well over time.

Ruane may sit on the sidelines when stocks have overheated, but when he believes strongly in a stock, he's willing to bet big. For example, Berkshire Hathaway at times makes up around 30% of the fund's assets. Other companies also often make up a big piece of the Sequoia pie. Ruane is usually comfortable with these large positions because of the wide margin of safety he requires before investing. Even if things turn bad temporarily, the margin usually acts as a cushion, preventing any significant losses—this is value investing at its best.

The Bottom Line

There are certainly other investors who deserve a spot in the Investor's Hall of Fame; however, the common threads remain the same. Each of the investors we've mentioned, and several others, are not afraid to challenge the conventional wisdoms of investing. Each looks for solid companies that have strong competitive advantages and looks to invest in these companies for a long period of time. And of course, the price they pay for their investments matters. In our opinion, these stock-pickers are on to something.

More Greats

Here's a list of a few other smart investors and where you can learn more about them.

Ron Baron—www.baronfunds.com

Christopher Davis—www.davisfunds.com

Jean-Marie Eveillard—www.firsteaglefunds.com

Mario Gabelli—www.gabelli.com

Mason Hawkins—www.longleafpartners.com

Bob Rodriguez—www.fpafunds.com

John Rogers—www.arielmutualfunds.com

Investor's Checklist

► Charlie Munger urges investors to gain a worldly wisdom to become successful at stock-picking.

► Bill Miller is known for often mixing traditional value plays with hyper-growth companies in his portfolio, as long as they are purchased at reasonable prices.

► Marty Whitman can usually be found rummaging through the rubble of distressed stocks—those of beaten-down companies, some on the brink of insolvency.

► Bill Nygren looks for stocks where 80% of the commentary about a company revolves around a piece of the company's business that contributes only about 20% of the profits.

► Ralph Wanger looks for value among small, under-followed companies with solid businesses and high growth.

► Bill Ruane studied under Ben Graham at Columbia University and even worked for him for a while. He's not afraid to hold concentrated positions nor cash when the situation is right.

Quiz

1   Which one of these investors studied under Ben Graham?

Answers to this quiz can be found on page 179

a	Bill Ruane.
b	Bill Nygren.
c	Ralph Wanger.

2   Which investor is known for mixing fast-growing Internet stocks with slower-growing industrials?

a	Marty Whitman.
b	Charlie Munger.
c	Bill Miller.

3   Which investor looks for small-cap growth stocks but won't pay too high a valuation?

a	Ralph Wanger.
b	Warren Buffett.
c	Marty Whitman.

4   If the media is constantly harping on a business that is responsible for only 5% of the sales and profits of a given company, who is most likely to have his interest piqued in that company?

a	Bill Ruane.
b	Bill Nygren.
c	Charlie Munger.

5   Which of the following is the common thread among all the great investors highlighted in this chapter?

a	They all hold Ph.D. degrees.
b	They all buy beaten-down companies that are on the ropes.
c	They all are focused on the price they are paying for their investments.

Worksheet

Answers to this worksheet can be found on page 190

1   Write down the name of the great investor most likely to be associated with the following:

> A. Reading a history book:

> B. Buying a company that has a major short-term issue:

> C. Making a single company 25% of his portfolio:

> D. Buying a stock that has no Wall Street analysts covering it:

> E. Hanging out with Warren Buffett:

> F. Buying a three-year-old company that is growing fast:

> G. Avoiding a stock because he doesn't trust a company's management:

> H. Seeing a trend and acting on an investment theme:

2   Name three of the things all the investors named in this chapter have in common:

> 1.

> 2.

> 3.

3   Explain Charlie Munger's idea of worldly wisdom.

4   Read some of the letters to shareholders from one or more of the investors mentioned in this lesson. What are some of the insights you have gleaned?

Rounding Out Your Portfolio

Lesson 310: Constructing a Portfolio

"The more constraints one imposes, the more one frees one's self. And the arbitrariness of the constraint serves only to obtain precision of execution."—Igor Stravinsky

Now that you've learned how to analyze companies and pick stocks, it is time to focus on putting groups of stocks together to construct your stock portfolio. While Nobel prizes have been awarded and entire books written about this topic, we'll try to briefly summarize the academic theory and focus on some of the more important aspects of portfolio management.

Though we will supply some guidance, no one answer is right for everyone when it comes to portfolio construction. It's more art than science. And perhaps that's why many believe portfolio management may be the difference that separates a great investor from an average mutual fund manager. Famed international stock-picker John Templeton has often said that he's right about his stock picks only about 60% of the time. Nevertheless, he has accumulated one of the best track records in the business. That's because great managers have a tendency to have more money invested in their big winners and less in their losers.

While we don't own any secret recipe to be able to tell you which stocks will be the big winners in your portfolio, we can guide you in deciding how many stocks you may need to own and some other considerations.

The Fat-Pitch Approach

In Lesson 301 of this book, we introduced you to the concept of the fat-pitch approach. We noted that you should hold relatively few great companies, purchased at a large margin of safety, and that you shouldn't be afraid to hold cash when you can't find good stocks to buy. But why?

The more stocks you hold, the lower your chances of underperforming the market. Of course, the more stocks you hold, the lower your chances of outperforming the market, but your portfolio is less risky. So the key question to ask yourself is: "Why do I invest in individual stocks at all?"

If the answer is that you think you can do better than a mutual fund, then you should hold a fairly concentrated portfolio of stocks because that gives you the highest odds of outperforming the averages. By "fairly concentrated," we mean 12 to 20 stocks.

As we previously noted, most investors will discover only a few good ideas in any given year—maybe five or six, sometimes a few more. Investors who hold more than 20 stocks at a time are often buying shares of companies they don't know much about, and then diversifying away the risk by holding lots of different names. It's tough to stray very far from the average return when you hold that many stocks, unless you have wacky weightings like 10% of your portfolio in one stock and 2% in each of the other 45.

What Do the Academics Say?

While we disagree with many aspects of modern portfolio theory, we do believe it contains some important frameworks that may help you to feel comfortable when investing in a concentrated portfolio. One of them involves the two ways to define risk:

Unsystematic risk is the unique risk of the company or stock that can be offset through diversification. Think of this as risk specific to a company, such as poor management, eroding profits, or a product recall.

Systematic risk is the market risk that cannot be diversified. This is the risk that affects the valuation of all stocks.

Number of Stocks in a Portfolio and the Standard Deviation of Portfolio Return

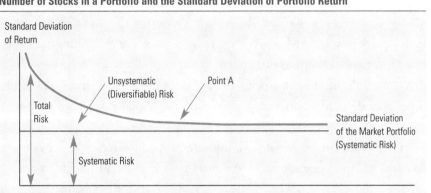

Source: Frank Reilly and Keith Brown, *Investment Analysis and Portfolio Management,* 7th Edition

In the figure above, what the academics have proven is that of your total risk, you can diversify away your unsystematic risk. The larger the number of stocks you own (horizontal axis), the more diversified you are, and the less unsystematic risk that you incur. For instance, if the profits of one of your companies are falling below expectations, and if you hold a large number of stocks, chances are another company in your portfolio is exceeding expectations.

There is some risk that you can't diversify away, the systematic risk. You cannot eliminate the risk from the macroeconomic factors that affect all stocks. So even if you own 1,000 stocks, you will not diversify away the inherent risk of owning stocks.

How Many Stocks Diversify Unsystematic Risk?

As the figure above shows, once you own enough stocks to reach point A, you have eliminated all the unsystematic risk. When you have reached this point, there is no need to own any more stocks to diversify your risk of concentration, that is, the unique risks associated with any one stock. So how many stocks do you need to own to reach point A?

Let's hear from the experts. In their book *Investment Analysis and Portfolio Management*, Frank Reilly and Keith Brown reported that in one set of studies for randomly selected stocks, "…about 90% of the maximum benefit of diversification was derived from portfolios of 12 to 18 stocks." In other words, if you own about 12 to 18 stocks, you have obtained more than 90% of the benefits of diversification, assuming you own an equally weighted portfolio.

Essentially, the theory says that if you are properly diversified, on average, you will get the same return in the market as if you had bought a passive market index. So if you want to obtain a higher return than the markets, you increase your chances by being less diversified. At the same time, you also increase your risk.

It is also important to note that if you own more than 18 stocks, you will have achieved almost full diversification, but now you will just have to keep track of more stocks in your portfolio for not much marginal benefit.

While much of academia has focused on the risk of not being diversified enough, we believe that there's a practical risk to being too diversified. When you own too many companies, it becomes nearly impossible to know your companies really well. Instead of having a competitive insight, you begin to run the risk of missing things. You may miss something important in the 10-k, skip on investigating the firm's second competitor, and so on. When you lose your focus and move outside your circle of competence, you lose your competitive advantage as an investor. Instead of playing with weak opponents for big stakes, you begin to become the weak opponent.

Non-Market Risk and a Concentrated Portfolio

Interestingly, holding a concentrated portfolio is not as risky as one may think. Just holding two stocks instead of one eliminates 46% of your unsystematic risk. Using a twist on the 80/20 rule of thumb, holding only eight stocks will eliminate about 81% of your diversifiable risk.

Unsystematic Risk and the Number of Stocks in a Portfolio

Number of Stocks	Non-Market Risk Eliminated (%)	Number of Stocks	Non-Market Risk Eliminated (%)
1	0	16	93
2	46	32	96
4	72	500	99
8	81	9,000	100

Source: Joel Greenblatt, *You Can Be a Stock Market Genius*

What about range of returns? Joel Greenblatt in his book *You Can Be a Stock Market Genius* explains that during one period that he examined, the average return of the stock market was about 10% and statistically, the one-year range of returns for a market portfolio (holding scores of stocks) in this period was between negative 8% and positive 28% about two-thirds of the time. That means that one-third of the time, the returns fell outside this 36-point range.

Interestingly, Greenblatt noted that if your portfolio is limited to only five stocks, the expected return remains 10%, but your one-year range expands to between negative 11% and positive 31% about two-thirds of the time. If there are eight stocks, the range is between negative 10% and positive 30%. In other words, it takes fewer stocks to diversify a portfolio than one might intuitively think.

Portfolio Weighting

In addition to knowing how many stocks to own in your portfolio and which stocks to buy, the percentage of your portfolio occupied by each stock is just as important. Unfortunately, the science and academics behind this important topic are scarce, and therefore, portfolio weighting is, again, more art than science.

We do know that the great money managers have a knack for having a greater percentage of their money in stocks that do well and a lesser amount in their bad picks. So how do they do it?

Essentially, a portfolio should be weighted in direct proportion to how much confidence you have in each pick. If you have a lot of confidence in the long-term outlook and the valuation of a stock, then it should be weighted more heavily than a stock you may be taking a flier on.

If a stock has a 10% weighting in your portfolio, then a 20% change in its price will move your overall portfolio 2%. If a stock has only a 3% weighting, a 20% price change has only a 0.6% effect on your portfolio. Weight your portfolio wisely. Don't be too afraid to have some big weightings, but be certain that the highest-weighted stocks are the ones you feel the most confident about. And of course, don't go off the deep end by having, for example, 50% of your portfolio in a single stock.

Portfolio Turnover

If you follow the fat-pitch method, you won't trade very often. Wide-moat companies selling at a discount are rare, so when you find one, you should pounce. Over the years, a wide-moat company will generate returns on capital higher than its cost of capital, creating value for shareholders. This shareholder value translates into a higher stock price over time.

If you sell after making a small profit, you might not get another chance to buy the stock, or a similar high-quality stock, for a long time. For this reason, it's irrational to quickly move in and out of wide-moat stocks and incur capital gains taxes and transaction costs. Your results, after taxes and trading expenses, likely won't be any better and may be worse. That's why many of the great long-term investors display low turnover in their portfolios. They've learned to let their winners run and to think like owners, not traders.

Circle of Competence and Sector Concentration

If you are investing within your circle of competence, then your stock selections will gravitate toward certain sectors and investment styles. Maybe you work in the medical field and thus are familiar with and own a number of pharmaceutical and biotechnology stocks. Or perhaps you've been educated in the Warren Buffett school of investing and cling to entrenched, easy-to-understand businesses such as Coca-Cola and Wrigley.

Following the fat-pitch strategy, you will naturally be overweight in some areas you know well and have found an abundance of good businesses. Likewise, you may avoid other areas where you don't know much or find it difficult to locate good businesses.

However, if all your stocks are in one sector, you may want to think about the effects that could have on your portfolio. For instance, you probably wouldn't want all of your investments to be in unattractive areas such as the airline or auto industry.

Adding Mutual Funds to a Stock Portfolio

In-the-know investors buy stocks. Those less-in-the-know, or those who choose to know less, own mutual funds. At least that's the rap when it comes to the stocks versus funds issue.

Maybe you can name all of your stocks and mutual funds off the top of your head and detail how each is currently valued. Good for you. But can you explain how they work together? Which are your core investments? Are you diversified? Do you have a lot of overlap? To answer these questions, Morningstar.com members can use our free "Instant X-Ray" tool. You'll discover your portfolio's asset mix, style-box breakdown, sector weightings, regional exposure, and much more.

Discover What You Own

But investing doesn't have to be a choice between investing directly in stocks or indirectly through mutual funds. Investors can—and many should—do both. The trick is determining how your portfolio can benefit most from each type of investment. Figuring out your appropriate stock/fund mix is (you knew this was coming) up to you.

Begin by looking for gaps in your portfolio and circle of competence. Do you have any foreign exposure? Do your assets cluster in particular sectors or style-box positions? Consider investing in mutual funds to gain exposure to countries and sectors that your portfolio currently lacks.

Some funds invest in micro-caps, others invest around the globe, still others focus on markets, such as real estate, that have their own quirks. Stock investors who turn over some of their dollars to an expert in these areas gain exposure to new opportunities without having to learn a whole new set of analytical skills.

For example, there are several ways to invest internationally:

- Purchase U.S. stocks like Wrigley and Coca-Cola that have extensive international operations.
- Purchase international stocks that have U.S. listings or ADRs such as Cadbury Schweppes and Unilever.
- Purchase international stocks on a foreign exchange.
- Own an international equity mutual fund.

Ultimately, your choice depends on your circle of competence and comfort level. While many may feel comfortable with picking their own international stocks, others may prefer to own an international equity fund.

The Bottom Line

Modern portfolio theory has been built on the assumption that you can't beat the stock market. If you can't beat the market portfolio, then the best you can do is to match the market's performance. Therefore, academic theory revolves around how to build the most efficient portfolio to match the market.

We have taken a different approach. Our objective is to outperform the market. Therefore, we believe that our odds increase by holding (not actively trading) relatively concentrated portfolios of between 12 and 20 great companies purchased with a margin of safety. The circle of competence will be unique to every person; therefore, your stock portfolio will naturally have sector, style, and country biases. If lacking in any area such as international stocks, a good mutual fund can be used to balance your overall portfolio.

Investor's Checklist

► Systematic risk is the risk of investing in stocks as an asset class. You cannot eliminate systematic risk through diversification.

► Unsystematic risk is the risk faced by owning individual companies. This risk can be reduced via diversification.

► Ninety percent of the benefits of diversification are achieved from holding 12 to 18 stocks. The marginal benefit from holding more stocks is minimal.

► Portfolio weighting is important to performance, and it is more art than science. Don't be too afraid to have some large weightings, but be certain that the highest-weighted stocks are the ones you feel the most confident about.

► Stay within your circle of competence when buying stocks and consider using a good mutual fund to plug holes in your portfolio.

Quiz

Answers to this quiz can be found on page 180

1   How many stocks do you need to own in your portfolio to derive 90% of the benefits from diversification?

a	5 to 10.
b	12 to 18.
c	80 to 100.

2   Unsystematic risk can be diversified away by:

a	It can't be diversified away.
b	Holding a larger number of stocks.
c	Holding bonds and cash.

3   You can increase your odds of beating the stock market index performance by:

a	Holding more than 40 stocks in your portfolio.
b	Holding less than 20 stocks in your portfolio.
c	The number of stocks in your portfolio doesn't matter.

4   By holding a concentrated portfolio, your returns will be better than the stock market:

a	All the time.
b	None of the time.
c	Some of the time.

5   What's the largest potential problem with owning too few stocks?

a	You may miss out on next year's best-performing stock.
b	You will be swinging only at fat pitches.
c	You run the risk that one bad stock pick could produce an extremely large loss.

Worksheet

1   Christine holds a portfolio of 20 stocks. However, she has insights into consumer and finance companies and therefore all of the companies in her portfolio are consumer and finance firms. Do you think she is properly diversified?

Answers to this worksheet can be found on page 190

2   Ron holds a portfolio of 10 stocks worth $100,000 and four large-blend equity mutual funds worth $100,000. He recently observed that many great mutual fund managers hold between 20 and 40 stocks. Ron is wondering if he should increase his stock portfolio by at least another 10 stocks in order to be fully diversified. What do you think?

3   Maria holds 20 U.S. stocks in her portfolio but is thinking that it might make sense to diversify internationally. What are some of her options?

Lesson 311: Introduction to Options

"There are two times in a man's life when he should not speculate: when he can't afford it and when he can."—Mark Twain

The large sums of money that can be won or lost over a fairly short period with options make them both intriguing and frightening to many investors. Because of the broad array of esoteric terms and unfamiliar concepts associated with them, options can be a difficult subject for investors to understand. Frankly, we don't think options are for everyone. In fact, many investors have had quite successful investing careers without ever considering them.

Even if you never end up buying or selling an option, it's a large enough part of the equities market to merit being aware of. You will probably be tempted at some point in your investing career to "take the next step" and leverage your ideas. This chapter will teach you the basics so you know what you may be getting into.

Call and Put Options on Stocks

At the heart of all the spreads and strategies discussed about options is the call and put. A call gives its owner the option to buy a stock at a specific price, known as the strike price, over a given period of time. A put provides the owner the option to sell a stock at a specific price (also called the strike price), over a given period of time. Let's look at how options are typically represented for a particular stock:

JUN07 50c

This refers to a call option with a strike price of $50 that expires in June 2007. The owner of this call would have the option to purchase the stock for $50 anytime before the option expires in June 2007.

AUG08 75p

This refers to a put option with a strike price of $75 that expires in August 2008. The owner of this put would have the option to sell the stock for $75 anytime before the option expires in August 2008.

What Is an Option Contract?

Options are traded in units called contracts. Each contract entitles the option buyer/owner to 100 shares of the underlying stock upon expiration. Thus, if you purchase seven call option contracts, you are acquiring the right to purchase 700 shares.

For every buyer of an option contract, there is a seller (also referred to as the writer of the option). In exchange for the cash received upon creating the option, the option writer gives up the right to buy or sell the underlying stock to someone else for the duration of the option. For instance, if the owner of a call option exercises his or her right to buy the stock at a particular price, the option writer must deliver the stock at that price.

Understanding Option Pricing

Two key phrases from our definitions for a call and put are "option to buy" and "option to sell." The owner of a call or put is not obligated to take any action. Thus, a call or put never has a value less than $0 before it expires. Consider the following example:

You own a call that gives you the right to buy a stock for $50. However, at expiration, the stock is priced at $45. Why would you exercise your right to purchase the stock for $50 when you can buy it for less in the stock market? You wouldn't. So, your call is worth $0 anytime the stock finishes below your strike price, which is $50 in this example.

When talking about option prices, people often refer to intrinsic value and premium to intrinsic value. (This intrinsic value has nothing to do with the intrinsic value we refer to when talking about the discounted cash flow of a company.) An option's intrinsic value is the difference between its strike price and the underlying stock price, when it favors the owner of the option. People often refer to intrinsic value as the amount that the option is "in the money." Let's look at three examples, assuming we are in 2006:

1. FEB07 60c when the stock is trading at $75

In this case, you own a call option that allows you to purchase the stock for $60 when it is trading for $75. We would say this call option has an intrinsic value of $15 because it gives you the right to purchase the stock for $15 less than you could purchase it for in the stock market.

2. OCT08 80p when the stock is trading at $50

In this case, you own a put option that allows you to sell the stock for $80 when it is trading for $50. We would say this put option has an intrinsic value of $30 because it gives you the right to sell the stock for $30 more than you could sell it for in the stock market.

3. JUL07 50c when the stock is trading for $40

In this case, you own a call option that allows you to buy the stock for $50 when it is trading for $40. This option has no intrinsic value. It is considered "out of the money."

Let's take a closer look at the third example above. Although it has no intrinsic value, we discover that the option is trading for about $2 in the marketplace. Why is that? Although the option isn't in the money now, there is still some time left (before expiration) for the stock to move such that it could place the option in the money. This is referred to as time value or option value.

In the case of the second example, the option may be trading for $32 even though the intrinsic value is only $30. In this case the option is trading at a $2 premium to its intrinsic value. This premium is also known as the time value.

Drivers of Option Value

There are several key factors that influence the value of an option. First, the level of volatility in the underlying stock plays a key role. The higher the stock's volatility, the greater the value of the option. If the underlying stock is more volatile, it means the option has a greater chance of trading in the money before the option expires.

Second, the amount of time left until the option expires influences the option's value. The more time left until expiration, the greater the value of the option. Again, the longer until expiration, the more time for an option to trade or finish in the money.

Finally, the direction the underlying stock trades will affect the value of the option. If a stock appreciates, it will positively affect call options and negatively impact put options. If a stock falls, it will have the opposite effect.

Basic Option Strategy—Leaps

There are literally scores of option strategies. Straddles, strangles, and butterflies are just some of the main types of strategies where an investor can use options (or sets of options) to bet on any number of stock and market movements. Most of these are beyond the scope of this workbook, so we will just focus on two strategies most often used by value investors.

First, leaps are options with relatively long time horizons, typically lasting for a year or two. (The term "leaps" is an acronym for "long-term equity anticipation securities.") Some value-oriented investors like call option leaps because they have such long time horizons and typically require less capital than buying the underlying stock.

For example, a stock may be trading for about $60, but the call options with two years to expiration and a $70 strike price may trade for $10. If an investor thinks the stock is worth $100 and will appreciate to that price before the leap expires, he or she could find the leap very attractive. Rather than spending $6,000 to purchase 100 shares of the stock, he or she could buy one leap contract for $1,000 (1 contract x $10 x 100). If the stock closes at $100 at expiration two years from now, the leap position would return $2,000 (1 contract x ($30 – $10) x 100). This would mark a $2,000 profit on a $1,000 investment (200%). However, if he or she had just purchased the stock, it would have marked a $4,000 profit on a $6,000 investment (67%).

Though each option is a right to buy or sell stock in lots of 100 shares, the actual price of the option is stated on a per-share basis. In other words, buying one contract at $2 would have a total cost of $200 ($2 x 100).

100 Times the Quote

As we see above, leaps can offer investors better returns. However, this bigger bang for the buck does not come without some additional risks. If the stock had finished at $70, the leap investor would have lost his/her $1,000 while the stock investor would have made $1,000. Also, the leap investor doesn't get to collect dividends, unlike the stock investor.

Let's also consider a case where this stock trades at $70 at the leap's expiration, but then goes up to $110 soon after expiration. The owner of the stock enjoys the appreciation to $110, but the option holder in our example is out of luck.

This latest example highlights perhaps the reason why options are a tough nut to crack for most investors. To be successful with options, you not only have to be correct about the direction of a stock's movement, you also have to be correct about the timing and magnitude of that movement. Deciding whether or not a company's stock is undervalued is difficult enough, and betting on when "Mr. Market" is going to be in one mood or the other adds great complexity.

Option Greeks

Industry professionals and academics have assigned various Greek letters to the different drivers of option value. We've listed some of the main "Greeks" below:

Δ **Delta** Measures how the option's value will respond to a change in the price of the underlying stock. Deltas range between negative 1 and 1. For example, a call option with a delta of 0.5 will increase $0.50 in value for every $1 increase in the price of the underlying stock.

Γ **Gamma** Measures how an option's delta changes as the price of the underlying stock changes. For example, a positive gamma implies that an option's delta will increase when the price of the underlying stock increases. A negative gamma implies that an option's delta will decrease when the underlying stock increases.

Θ **Theta** Measures the time value in an option. In particular, an option's theta tells you how much an option will decrease over the course of one day. So, if an option's theta were 0.05, it would imply that the option's value will decrease $0.05 per day from lost time value.

Vega The only "Greek" not represented by a real Greek letter, measures how the option's value responds to a change in the volatility of the underlying stock. For example, if an option's vega is 0.15, for every 1% increase in a stock's volatility the option will appreciate $0.15.

Another Strategy—Baby Puts

"Baby puts" refer to put options that are far out of the money, and therefore trade cheaply. Investors will sell these baby puts on stocks that they are comfortable purchasing at a specific price, which will be the strike price of the put they are selling. Typically, this is the price that builds in a margin of safety to their estimate of the stock's fair value.

For example, say an investor would be happy to purchase Coca-Cola for $35 per share, but the stock is trading at $45. It's currently January, and the investor notices that the May $35 put options are trading for $1. The investor decides to sell (write) the May $35 put options for $1. This means the investor collects $1 for selling the right to someone else to sell the investor the stock for $35 anytime before the option's May expiration date. So, if Coca-Cola stock doesn't fall below $35 by the May expiration, the investor pockets the $1. However, if the stock falls below $35 before May, the investor will probably be required to purchase Coca-Cola stock for $35, because the person to whom he or she sold the put option will exercise his or her right to sell the stock for $35.

Value investors might be willing to partake in this strategy because they decided in advance that $35 was a good price to purchase Coca-Cola stock. And, if the stock doesn't fall below $35, they get to collect $1 (by selling the baby put) as they wait for Coke's stock to trade cheaper.

This strategy is not without some fairly large risks. If the investor doesn't have enough cash in his or her account to purchase the stock, the investor's broker may require additional funds be deposited. We'd recommend considering this strategy only if an investor has plenty of cash on hand. Also, a fresh piece of news could surface (between the time the investor sells the put and the put expires) that might change the investor's opinion of the fair value of the stock.

Books on Options

This chapter was merely to get you acquainted with options. You will certainly need to read more on the subject before deciding whether to actually trade options. Below are some of the best books we've discovered.

Option Volatility & Pricing by Sheldon Natenberg, 1994. Published by McGraw-Hill. In our opinion, this is the first book one should read to learn more about options.

Options, Futures, and Other Derivatives by John C. Hull, revised 2002. Published by Prentice Hall. If you read Natenberg's book and grasped everything he had to say, Hull's book may interest you as a follow-up. It's far more technical, in our opinion, and we'd recommend it only for those serious about really digging into options.

A cheap and easy way to learn more about options is to request an option brochure from your broker. Brokers typically provide these pamphlets free of charge. These readings cover most of the basics on options.

The Bottom Line

Some investors like options because they require less capital and thereby offer potentially greater returns. Others like to use them to execute strategies like the "baby put" example above. However, options also possess risks that will repel many investors, and rightfully so, in our opinion. Like we mentioned earlier, one can have a very successful investing career without spending a moment thinking about options. But for those interested in understanding these types of investments, we suggest working through our examples and reading more from one of the authors we recommend.

Investor's Checklist

▶ A call option gives you the right to purchase a stock for a specific price (the strike price) over a set period of time (until the option expires). You are not obligated to purchase the stock at the strike price, so you will exercise your option only if the strike price is cheaper than the stock's market price. This is why a call option is never worth less than $0 before expiration.

▶ A put option gives you the right to sell a stock for a specific price (the strike price) over a set period of time (until the option expires). You are not obligated to sell the stock at the strike price, so you will exercise your option only if the strike price is higher than the stock's market price. This is why a put option is never worth less than $0 before expiration.

▶ The value of an option increases as the volatility of the underlying stock increases. Thus, more volatile stocks tend to have more expensive options associated with them.

▶ Options with more time left until expiration are more valuable. Be mindful of the time left until expiration when considering an option.

▶ Leaps are one way value investors have used options historically. Leaps have long periods of time before they expire. This gives value investors a longer horizon for their investment ideas to play out.

▶ Many investors have had successful investing careers without ever considering options.

Quiz

1   If the JAN07 60c is priced at $10 and the stock is trading for $67, what is the option's intrinsic value?

a	$7.
b	$3.
c	$60.

Answers to this quiz can be found on page 180

2   If the DEC06 45c is priced at $5 and the stock is trading for $44, what is the option's time value?

a	$0.
b	$5.
c	$1.

3   If an option, currently priced at $2, has a theta of 0.25, and the underlying stock has no change in value, what should be the option's price tomorrow?

a	$2.25.
b	$0.25.
c	$1.75.

4   If you purchase five call option contracts on a given stock, how many shares of stock will you have the right to purchase at expiration?

a	500.
b	5.
c	50.

5   Which of the following is not true?

a	You can be a successful investor even if you never buy or sell an option.
b	Leap options can create much greater returns with lower risk than stocks.
c	When buying options, the timing of the underlying stock price movements is just as important as the direction of the movement.

Worksheet

Answers to this worksheet can be found on page 191

1   If you were interested in purchasing Wal-Mart stock for $45, but it is currently trading for $50, how could you use put options to collect money as you wait for the stock to fall to $45 or lower?

2   If you think a stock is going to increase in value over the next year, although it may become more highly volatile over the coming year as well, what may be one strategy to consider?

3   What does the following notation represent: MAR07 75c

4   How much money would it cost to buy 10 contracts of the JAN06 55c priced at $7.50?

Lesson 312: Unconventional Equities

"They give you cash, which is just as good as money."—*Yogi Berra*

Our discussion of the stock market would not be complete without an examination of what we might refer to as "unconventional equities." We lump three types of securities into this category: real estate investment trusts (REITs), master limited partnerships (MLPs), and royalty trusts. These securities trade like stocks but carry important differences, particularly with regard to tax treatment. Let's take a look at the benefits and drawbacks of each security type.

Real Estate Investment Trusts (REITs)

A real estate investment trust (REIT) is a company that owns and manages income-producing real estate. REITs were created by an act of Congress in 1960 to enable large and small investors alike to enjoy the rental income from commercial property. REITs are governed by many regulations, the most important being that they must distribute at least 90% of their taxable income to shareholders each year as dividends; the REIT is permitted to deduct dividends paid to shareholders from its taxable income. Other important regulations include:

▸ Asset requirements: at least 75% of assets must be real estate, cash, and government securities.
▸ Income requirements: at least 75% of gross income must come from rents, interest from mortgages, or other real estate investments.
▸ Stock ownership requirements: shares in the REIT must be held by a minimum of 100 shareholders.

REITs can be public or private. There are nearly 200 publicly traded REITs in the U.S. with a total market cap of about $300 billion. These REITs are divided into three major categories depending on the type of assets they own: equity

REITs own and manage properties, mortgage REITs lend money to property owners directly or indirectly through mortgage-backed securities, and hybrid REITs own property directly and lend money to real estate owners.

REITs specialize by property type. They invest in most major property types with nearly two-thirds of investment being in offices, apartments, shopping centers, regional malls, and industrial facilities. The rest is divided among hotels, self-storage facilities, health-care properties, and some specialty REITs that own anything from prisons, theatres, and golf courses to timberlands.

Benefits of REITs

High Yields. For many investors, the main attraction of REITs is their dividend yield. The average long-term (15-year) dividend yield for REITs is about 8%, well more than the yield of the S&P 500 Index. (The S&P 500 yielded roughly 2% at this writing.) Also, REIT dividends are secured by stable rents from long-term leases, and many REIT managers employ conservative leverage on the balance sheet.

Capital Gains. In addition to the growing, secure dividend yield, REITs have historically appreciated in value, providing decent capital gains. This has led to respectable annual total returns of about 12% historically. The last five years before mid-2005 have been exceptional for REITs, which produced total returns of 23% while other major stock indexes produced negative returns.

Simple Tax Treatment. Unlike most partnerships, tax issues for REIT investors are fairly straightforward. Each year, REITs send Form 1099-DIV to their shareholders, containing a breakdown of the dividend distributions. For tax purposes, dividends are allocated to ordinary income, capital gains, and return of capital. As REITs do not pay taxes at the corporate level, investors are taxed at their individual tax rate for the ordinary income portion of the dividend. The portion of the dividend taxed as capital gains arises if the REIT sells assets. Return of capital, or net distributions in excess of the REIT's earnings and profits, are not taxed as ordinary income, but instead applied to reduce the shareholder's cost basis in the stock. When the shares are eventually sold, the difference between the share price and reduced tax basis is taxed as a capital gain.

Liquidity of REIT Shares. REIT shares are bought and sold on a stock exchange. By contrast, buying and selling property directly involves higher expenses and requires a great deal of effort.

Diversification. Studies have shown that adding REITs to a diversified investment portfolio increases returns and reduces risk since REITs have little correlation with the S&P 500.

Drawbacks of REITs

Sensitive to Demand for Other High-Yield Assets. Generally, rising interest rates could make Treasury securities more attractive, drawing funds away from REITs and lowering their share prices.

Property Taxes. REITs must pay property taxes, which can make up as much as 25% of total operating expenses. State and municipal authorities could increase property taxes to make up for budget shortfalls, reducing cash flows to shareholders.

Tax Rates. One of the downsides to the high yield of REITs is that taxes are due on dividends, and the tax rates are typically higher than the 15% most dividends are currently taxed at. This is because a large chunk of a REIT's dividends (typically about three quarters, though it varies widely by REIT) is considered ordinary income, which is usually taxed at a higher rate.

Analyzing a REIT

1 Dividend yield: A high dividend yield is not always a good thing. Many REITs with above-average yields—compared with their peer averages—have recently cut their dividends due to temporary setbacks in cash flow or because of debt covenants limiting dividend payments.

2 Dividend security: The amount of leverage—measured by debt to total market capitalization—should generally be 50% or less. Other measures of dividend security include the dividend coverage ratio—the higher the better—and the FFO dividend payout ratio—the lower the better. (See below for more on FFO.)

3 Funds from operations (FFO): This is a supplemental measure of earnings adopted by the REIT community to address the fact that net income does not capture a REIT's cash-flow-generating ability. Basically, FFO is net income plus real estate depreciation less any gains from property sales.

4 Earnings growth: The key measure is FFO per share growth, as REITs typically issue a lot of equity to make up for the fact that they have little cash left over to finance growth after distributing most of their earnings as dividends.

5 Net asset value (NAV): This is an estimate of the current market value of a REIT's properties. Book value has little relevance for evaluating REITs, as it does not capture the future earning capacity of a REIT's properties.

Master Limited Partnerships (MLPs)

In recent years, many U.S. energy firms have reorganized their slow-growing, yet stable businesses, such as pipelines and storage terminals, into master limited partnerships, or MLPs. There are some important differences between buying shares of a corporation and buying a stake in an MLP. With MLPs, investors buy units of the partnership, rather than shares of stock, and are referred to as "unitholders."

There are two classes of MLP owner: general partners and limited partners. General partners manage the day-to-day operations of the partnership. An MLP technically has no employees, so all services, from management to book-keeping, are provided by the general partner. All other investors are limited partners and have no involvement in the partnership's operations. Limited-partner units are publicly traded, while general-partner units usually are not.

The general partner stake is often 2% of the partnership, though the general partner can also own limited-partner units to increase its percentage of ownership.

Companies that use the MLP format tend to operate in very stable, slow-growing industries, such as pipelines. These types of firms usually offer dim prospects for unit price appreciation, but the stability of the industries that use the MLP format means below-average risk for investors. Cash distributions usually stay relatively steady over time (growing at little more than overall inflation), causing MLP units to trade somewhat like bonds, rising when interest rates fall and vice versa.

Benefits of MLPs

High Yield. Most MLPs offer very attractive yields, generally falling in the 6%-7% range.

Consistent Distributions Over Time. The businesses operated as MLPs tend to be very stable and produce consistent cash flows year after year, making the cash distributions on MLP units very predictable.

Favorable Tax Treatment. Firms primarily switch to the MLP structure to avoid taxes. While shareholders in a corporation face double taxation—paying taxes first at the corporate level, and then at the personal level when those earnings are received as dividends—owners of a partnership are taxed only once: when they receive distributions. There is no partnership equivalent of corporate income tax. Cash distributions to owners often exceed partnership income, and when they do, the difference is counted as a return of capital to the limited partner and taxed at the capital gains rate when the unitholder sells. Not only are capital gains deferred until an owner decides to sell, but capital gains tax rates are lower than income tax rates.

Lower Cost of Capital. The absence of taxes at the company level gives MLPs a lower cost of capital than is typically available to corporations, allowing the MLPs to pursue projects that might not be feasible for a taxable entity.

General Partner Compensation Aligned with Limited Partners' Interest. Most general partners are paid on a sliding scale, receiving a greater share of each dollar of cash flow as the limited partners' cash distributions rise, giving the general partner an incentive to increase limited-partner distributions.

!

Splitting MLP Cash Distributions	Most MLPs pay out cash using a tiered system. For example, the general partner of Houston-based Enterprise Products Partners receives 2% of quarterly distributions up to $0.253 per common unit, 15% for the distributions between $0.254 and $0.3085 per unit, and 25% if the distributions are above $0.3085.
	At many MLPs, the top tier provides for distributions to the general partner at a 50% marginal rate. While a higher top tier leaves less cash for limited partners, it also gives the general partner extra incentive to maintain cash flow and not cut distributions since the general partner would lose out just as much as limited partners.

Drawbacks of MLPs

Personal Tax Liability. Each unitholder is responsible for paying his or her share of the partnership's income taxes, which can make filing taxes more complicated. This is particularly true for larger unitholders, who may have to pay taxes in the various states in which the partnership operates. Moreover, limited partners might owe taxes on partnership income even if the units are held in a retirement account.

Limited Pool of Investors. MLPs face a smaller pool of potential investors than traditional equities because institutional investors, such as pension funds, are not allowed to hold MLP units without incurring tax liability. These large investors do not ordinarily pay taxes, so they tend to shy away from MLPs.

Institutional investors represent the majority of investor dollars in the market, so eliminating them reduces the potential demand for MLP units. Congress recently approved a provision allowing mutual funds to buy MLPs, which should dramatically increase the number of potential investors.

Royalty Trusts

Royalty trusts, like MLPs, generally invest in energy sector assets. Unlike the steady cash flows at MLPs, royalty trusts generate income from the production of natural resources such as coal, oil, and natural gas. These cash flows are subject to swings in commodity prices and production levels, which can cause them to be very inconsistent from year to year. The trusts have no physical operations of their own and have no management or employees. Rather, they are merely financing vehicles that are run by banks, and they trade like stocks. Other companies mine the resources and pay royalties on those resources to the trust. For example, Burlington Resources, an oil exploration and production company, is the operator for the assets that the largest U.S. royalty trust, San Juan Basin Royalty Trust, owns the royalties on.

Royalty trusts end up on most investors' radar screens because of the incredibly high yields some of them offer, many in excess of 10%. In a low-interest-rate environment, it's easy to understand why such an income-producing investment might be garnering more attention.

Many of the positive and negative attributes of owning a royalty trust are similar to those faced by MLP unitholders.

Benefits of Royalty Trusts

High Yield. Trusts are required to pay out essentially all of their cash flow as distributions. Because of this, nearly all royalty trusts have above-average yields, many wildly above average.

Tax-Advantaged Yield. Due to depreciation and depletion, distributions from most trusts are not considered income in the eyes of the IRS. Rather, these nonincome distributions are used to reduce an owner's cost basis in the stock, which is then taxed at the lower capital gains rate and is deferred until an owner sells.

No Corporate Income Tax. Trusts are merely "pass-through" investment vehicles. The issues surrounding double taxation of dividends do not apply.

Peculiar Tax Credits. Have you ever received a tax credit for producing fuels from nonconventional sources? If you own a royalty trust, you might qualify for such credits. The laws on this issue are in flux, and the credits are generally small, but it's still a nice potential perk.

"Pure" Bets on Commodities. Want to bet on the future price appreciation of natural gas but don't want to get involved with the futures market? An excellent way to do that would be to buy a royalty trust that owns gas. The value of any given trust and the distributions it pays are directly tied to the prices of the underlying commodity. Just remember the sword cuts both ways here. The trust's income (and therefore probably the trust's stock price) could end up falling if commodity prices go down instead of up.

Drawbacks of Royalty Trusts

Depletion, Depletion, Depletion. Royalty trusts own royalties on a finite amount of resources. Once those resources are gone, they're gone. As the resources deplete, royalties and distributions will fall and will, eventually, go to zero. In financial terms, there is no terminal value. Granted, most trusts won't hit this point for two or three decades (or more), but it's still incredibly important to consider that distributions will eventually contract and disappear.

Volatile Distributions. Trusts typically pay out their distributions on a quarterly or monthly basis. If royalties fall in that period due to the underlying commodity price tanking, distributions will also fall. It's entirely conceivable that a trust that yielded 15% in the last 12 months could yield 3% in the next 12.

Our discussion here has focused on trusts based in the U.S., but royalty trusts are a much bigger deal in Canada. In fact, many Canadian companies, including several not associated with natural resources, are contemplating switching to the trust structure in order to reap the tax benefits.

There are some key differences between American and Canadian trusts. Perhaps the most important has to do with their capital structures. American trusts are extremely static. When a trust is created, the assets it has are generally the only assets it will ever have, and trusts typically do not take on debt. Meanwhile, Canadian trusts are much more dynamic, with the ability to raise debt and equity capital to purchase additional assets and grow over time.

Canadian Trusts

Tax-Filing Complexity. Owners of royalty trusts are required to report the pro rata portion of a trust's total income and expenses on their tax returns. This typically means filing Schedules E and B as well as having additional work with Form 1040.

State Income Taxes. Owners of trusts are liable for paying income taxes in the states in which the trust generates its royalties. Different states have different thresholds for when taxes have to actually be filed and paid, and the likelihood of owing income tax in multiple states increases with the size of a given ownership position.

The Bottom Line

Though they require a bit of work to understand and may increase tax complexity, investing in REITS, MLPS, and royalty trusts can boost the income-producing power of most portfolios.

▶ REITs, MLPs, and royalty trusts typically provide higher yields than traditional equities.

▶ REITs offer investors a highly liquid way to invest in real estate compared with investing in real estate directly.

▶ MLPs hold slow-growth energy assets like pipelines and storage terminals.

▶ Royalty trusts receive cash payments from their investment properties that produce natural resources, such as natural gas, coal, and oil.

▶ Cash distributions on MLPs and REITs tend to be more consistent than royalty trusts because the cash flows they generate are steadier.

▶ Owning MLPs or royalty trusts can increase tax-filing complexity.

Quiz

1   Which of the following is not an advantage of each of the unconventional equities discussed in this chapter?

Answers to this quiz can be found on page 181

a	Company tax advantages.
b	High yields.
c	Stable cash flows.

2   Which of the following is true regarding the tax treatment of MLPs?

a	All taxes are deferred until the units are sold.
b	The owner might have to file tax returns in the states where the partnership operates.
c	MLP unitholders pay regular income tax on the full amount of any cash distributions received during the year.

3   Which type of security provides the most exposure to commodity markets?

a	Royalty trusts.
b	REITs.
c	MLPs.

4   The prices of MLP units often change in conjunction with changes in:

a	Oil prices.
b	Rents.
c	Interest rates.

5   Which of the following is not one of the benefits of owning REITs?

a	Returns on REITs have a low correlation with traditional stocks.
b	Real estate owned by an REIT does not have to pay property tax.
c	REITs are very liquid compared with owning real estate directly.

Worksheet

Answers to this worksheet can be found on page 192

1   Cozad Pipeline Partners, a fictional master limited partnership, paid $1.25 in cash distributions to unitholders last year. It reported net income of $0.35 per unit. Assuming an average regular tax rate of 25%, what would be an investor's tax liability for last year on 1,000 units? How much in distributions did this investor receive?

2   Mike is considering selling his holdings of Hastings Trust, a fictional royalty trust. He bought 600 shares for $35 each two years ago. In that time, the market price has risen to $40 while the trust has recognized $2.30 per share of net income and paid $9.30 per share in distributions. If Mike decides to sell, what would his capital gains tax liability be? Assume a capital gains tax rate of 15%.

3   Find the 2004 annual report for Boston Properties, a real REIT. What type of real estate does it invest in? Where is most of its real estate located? What was the dividend in each of the past five years? What percentage of Boston Properties' leases expire after 2014?

continued...

continued...

4   Arthur is trying to decide how to invest $10,000 in order to produce the most aftertax income. He plans to sell the investment in one year. Which of the following investments should he choose? Assume that his marginal income tax rate is 30%, the capital gains rate is 15%, and he expects to be able to sell the investment for a price equal to his purchase price. Net income, dividend, and distribution figures are per share/unit.

☐ **REIT:** 125 shares @ $80. Expected dividend of $6.40 per share (of which $4.00 is treated as ordinary income and $2.40 as return of capital), net income of $2.00.

☐ **MLP:** 200 units @ $50. Expected cash distribution of $3.50 per share, net income of $1.50.

☐ **Royalty trust:** 250 shares @ $40. Expected cash distribution of $3.60, all counted as a return of capital.

References

Additional Morningstar Resources

Morningstar isn't just about mutual funds anymore! In addition to this workbook series, Morningstar publishes a number of other products that can help you to become a better, more informed stock investor. These resources can be obtained at your local library, by calling Morningstar directly at 866-608-9570, or by visiting www.morningstar.com.

Morningstar.com

Our Web site features information on stocks, funds, bonds, retirement plans, and much more. In addition to powerful portfolio tools that make tracking investments easier, you'll find daily articles by Morningstar analysts. Much information on the site is free, and there is a reasonably priced Premium Membership service available. Premium Members receive access to more-powerful analytical tools as well as in-depth Analyst Reports (including star ratings and fair value estimates) on nearly 1,600 stocks.

Morningstar® Stocks 500™

Our annual book of full-page reports and unique Morningstar tools helps you uncover the best stock values around. Star ratings, economic moat ratings, fair value estimates, Stewardship Grades, and analyst-written reports make deciding when to buy and sell easy. *Morningstar Stocks 500* makes an excellent desktop reference for throughout the year.

Morningstar® StockInvestor™

StockInvestor is Morningstar's flagship monthly stocks newsletter. Each issue has 32 pages filled with model portfolios, opinions on headline stocks, "red flag" stocks to avoid, and watch lists of wide-moat stocks. To date, both model portfolios in the newsletter (the "Tortoise" and the "Hare") have outperformed the wider stock market, with the "Tortoise" beating it by a large margin.

Morningstar® DividendInvestor™

Interested in generating income from your stock investments? *DividendInvestor* focuses on showing you how to profit from the compound effect of dividends and growth. This monthly newsletter includes a model portfolio and an "On the Bench" watch list of dividend-paying firms worth keeping an eye on.

continued...

Morningstar® Growth Investor™

Now you can be a growth investor while minimizing the normally high risks associated with this style of investing. Our new newsletter helps you spot growth stocks when they can be had at great prices, thus reducing the downside risk. Each issue includes our Growth Portfolio, Growth Giants watch list, companies with Growth at Risk, and more.

The Five Rules for Successful Stock Investing™
Morningstar's Guide to Building Wealth and Winning in the Market

A perfect follow-up to the workbook series, this book, published in 2004, touches on a wide range of stock-related topics, including how to dig into financial statements, how to find great companies that will create shareholder wealth, and how to evaluate companies in all the major sectors. And, of course, it will give you the five rules we think every investor should follow.

Recommended Readings

This workbook series can certainly start you down the path of learning to become a great investor. But as with any intellectual exercise, it pays to both confirm what you've learned as well as to soak up as many other ideas and viewpoints as possible.

Below are what we believe to be some of the most relevant investing books today. These are what we Morningstar analysts have read in forming our own philosophy. We've included classics (*Security Analysis* and *The Intelligent Investor*) as well as those that are more timely and thought-provoking (*Moneyball* and *When Genius Failed*). All are worth reading.

We've tried to group the books since some are light reads easily accessible to new investors, while others require more concentration and experience in order to extract value.

Easy

The Only Investment Guide You'll Ever Need by Andrew Tobias, 2005 (revised). Published by Harvest Books. Maybe not the only guide you'll need, but this is an excellent introduction to investing in general. This book was originally published in 1978 with numerous revisions since then.

Stocks for the Long Run (Third Edition) and *The Future for Investors* by Jeremy J. Siegel, 2002 and 2005, respectively. Published by McGraw-Hill and Crown Business, respectively. Still wondering whether or not to invest in stocks? Professor Siegel's works plainly make the case for equities.

Buffett: The Making of an American Capitalist by Roger Lowenstein, 1996 (Reprint Edition). Published by Main Street Books. One of the many great Warren Buffett books available.

Of Permanent Value: The Story of Warren Buffett by Andrew Kilpatrick, 2005 (revised). Published by Andy Kilpatrick Pub Empire. Yet another excellent book on Warren Buffett and his company, Berkshire Hathaway.

One Up on Wall Street and *Beating the Street* by Peter Lynch, 2000 (Fireside Edition) and 1994, respectively. Published by Simon & Schuster. One of the best investors of his time, Lynch gives insights into how he goes about finding great investments. These are very accessible tomes.

continued...

Why Smart People Make Big Money Mistakes and How to Correct Them: Lessons from the New Science of Behavioral Economics by Gary Belsky and Thomas Gilovich, 2000. Published by Simon & Schuster. This easy read introduces the basics of how psychology and investing interact.

Moneyball by Michael Lewis, 2003. Published by W. W. Norton & Company. What can a book about baseball teach us about investing? This book illustrates how a team tries to find value that no one else sees.

Intermediate

The Essays of Warren Buffett: Lessons for Corporate America by Warren Buffett and Lawrence A. Cunningham, 2001. Published by The Cunningham Group. This book, one of our absolute favorites, contains a collection of Warren Buffett's letters to his shareholders. Buffett's intellect, integrity, and wit shine bright.

The Intelligent Investor: The Definitive Book on Value Investing, Revised Edition by Benjamin Graham and Jason Zweig, 2003. Published by HarperBusiness. The second of Graham's two classics, this book's wisdom still resonates decades after its first publication.

Common Stocks and Uncommon Profits by Philip A. Fisher with Kenneth L. Fisher, 2003 (revised). Published by Wiley. Rather than emphasize cheap stock prices, Fisher focuses on finding great companies that will grow profitably over many years. Buffett's philosophy can be called a marriage between Graham and Fisher. The first edition of this book was published in 1958.

Built to Last by Jim Collins and Jerry Porras, 2002. Published by HarperBusiness. By studying visionary companies, the authors try to find what characteristics great businesses share.

When Genius Failed: The Rise and Fall of Long-Term Capital Management by Roger Lowenstein, 2001. Published by Random House. This book chronicles the spectacular rise and fall of a large trading firm and highlights that no investor can completely beat back risk.

172

A Random Walk Down Wall Street by Burton G. Malkiel, 2004 (revised). Published by W. W. Norton & Company. This thought-provoking read makes the case for indexing and shows how much of what we attribute as brilliance among money managers may really be random chance.

Value Investing: From Graham to Buffett and Beyond by Bruce Greenwald, Judd Kahn, Paul Sonkin, and Michael van Biema, 2004 (revised). Published by Wiley. This book provides a solid overview of the value-investing philosophy, with profiles of some of the most prominent value investors.

Advanced

Security Analysis: The Classic 1934 Edition by Benjamin Graham and David Dodd, 1934 (republished 1996). Published by McGraw-Hill. This is quite simply the bible of fundamental value investing. It's a true classic, but not light reading.

Financial Statement Analysis: A Practitioner's Guide (Third Edition) by Martin Fridson and Fernando Alvarez, 2002. Published by Wiley. If you want to learn how to dig deeper into a company's financial statements, this is a good guide.

Valuation: Measuring and Managing the Value of Companies (Third Edition) by McKinsey & Company Inc., 2000. Published by Wiley. There are many books on how to value a company, and this is the one that has most often found its way onto Morningstar analysts' shelves.

Competitive Strategy by Michael E. Porter, 1998. Published by Free Press. Want to learn how to think more about competitive advantages and economic moats? This is a must-read.

Triumph of the Optimists: 101 Years of Global Investment Returns by Elroy Dimson, Paul Marsh, and Mike Staunton, 2002. Published by Princeton University Press. This book gives an excellent historical perspective into the long-run returns of a wide variety of investments from around the world.

Quiz 301: The Fat-Pitch Strategy

1   b.   Often there are too few fat-pitch opportunities to allow for a fully diversified portfolio. If investors purchase wide-moat companies with a sufficient margin of safety, and maintain a long-term investment horizon, we believe the risks associated with holding relatively few stocks in a portfolio can be greatly mitigated.

2   b.   It may be difficult to patiently sit on cash when the stock market is rising and you feel as if you're missing out on the fun. However, holding cash is akin to holding an option for when the market provides opportunities to buy at lower prices. If you're not finding any fat pitches in the market, it's probably because the market is priced too high; thus, cash is not a detriment because it's helping you refrain from "buying high" and "selling low" instead of the other way around.

3   a.   Wide-moat companies typically have long-term structural advantages over the competition. A wide-moat firm typically has a return on capital above its cost of capital. Also, just because a firm has a wide moat, that does not mean its stock price is always cheap. On the contrary, because wide-moat firms are typically very strong and stable, they often trade at premium prices. This is why you should not be afraid to swing away on those rare occasions a fat pitch does come your way.

4   b.   Although it's possible that you could purchase a stock that will never need to be sold, there are occasions that investors should sell stocks. The other two answers are both reasons that investors should not trade very often.

5   b.   The fat-pitch approach is best described as buying above-average (wide-moat) companies at prices that provide a margin of safety to your fair value estimate.

Quiz 302: Psychology and Investing

1   a.   Overconfident investors trade more rapidly because they think they know more than those on the opposite end of the trade.

2   b.   Investors often cling to investments in order to wait for a point at which they will break even, even if the underlying business has fundamentally changed for the worse.

coninued...

3   b.   Representativeness is a mental shortcut that causes investors to give too much weight to recent evidence—such as short-term performance numbers—and too little weight to evidence from the more distant past. For instance, a look at a company's profit trends over the past six years is likely to yield more insight than looking at that company's stock performance over the past six months.

4   a.   You may feel regret after a bad outcome, such as a stretch of weak performance from a given stock, even if you chose the investment for all the right reasons and the underlying business remains strong. Regret can lead you to make a bad sell decision.

5   c.   Following investment fashion can lead to fading performance or inappropriate investments for your particular goals.

Quiz 303: The Case for Dividends

1   b.   Dividend Yield = Dividend Per Share ÷ Stock Price

The calculation reads: ($0.30 × 4) ÷ $27.00 = 4.4%

Okay, we threw you a little bit of a curveball with that one. To obtain yield, we want to use the indicated (annualized) dividend rate. A $0.30 quarterly dividend should be multiplied by four before dividing by the stock price.

2   a.   The other two statements are possibly true—temporarily depressed earnings will inflate a firm's payout ratio, but 87% is a high number, and a firm that is paying out 87% of earnings probably doesn't have many reinvestment opportunities. However, the first answer—that 87% of dividends are guaranteed—is patently false. Dividends are never guaranteed.

3   c.   The sustainable growth rate is a hypothetical figure, not a guarantee of investment opportunities or dividend growth.

4   c.   Moats are critical both for the sustainability of a dividend and for its growth potential.

5   b.   Philip Morris, now named Altria, was the best-performing stock in the period, according to Siegel's research. Despite its core market being in decline the entire time, the company was extremely aggressive in paying dividends and buying back its shares.

Quiz 304: 20 Stock-Investing Tips

1   a.   Remember, the economics of a business usually trump the competence of management.

2   b.   While past performance is indeed no guarantee of future results, it is a pretty darn good indicator.

3   b.   You should tune out the noise, which includes short-term predictions made by others concerning things that can't be predicted.

4   a.   Willingness to go against the crowd and having a margin of safety are two of the common characteristics of great investors.

5   c.   Reading annual reports will help you know more about your companies, which will make you a better investor. By constantly looking at unrealized capital gains, you may be anchoring on an irrelevant data point—the price you paid—concerning the future value of a stock.

Quiz 305: Deep Value—Benjamin Graham

1   c.   Graham wrote *Security Analysis* and *The Intelligent Investor. Common Stocks and Uncommon Profits* was authored by Philip Fisher.

2   b.   Graham thought it was absolutely critical to buy stocks or bonds only when prices offered a margin of safety. Otherwise, you would not be protected against unforeseen events that may lead to permanent capital loss.

3   b.   Intrinsic value is the true worth of a business, which is entirely separate from its stock market price. The intrinsic value of a business is based on its balance sheet net worth and/or future earnings power, not on what participants in the market are willing to pay.

4   a.   Since stocks represent partial ownership of real businesses, the same behavior that makes sense in the business world makes sense in the stock market.

5   b.   According to Graham, an investment operation must involve thorough analysis, safety of principal, and an adequate return; otherwise the operation is speculative.

Quiz 306: Holding Superior Growth— Philip Fisher

1 c. Fisher's investment classic, *Common Stocks and Uncommon Profits*, was first published in 1958.

2 a. Fisher firmly believed that an investor's best shot at truly outstanding gains was to find a young, well-managed company with compelling growth prospects.

3 a. According to Fisher, the holding period for a well-selected stock is approximately forever.

4 a. Fisher believed in owning a concentrated portfolio of excellent companies.

5 a. For Fisher, there are only three reasons to sell a stock:
1) If you have made a serious mistake in your assessment of the company;
2) If the company no longer passes the 15 points as clearly as before;
3) If you could reinvest the money in another, far more attractive company.

Quiz 307: Great Companies at Reasonable Prices—Warren Buffett

1 b. Buffett rejects the idea that diversification is helpful to informed investors. He thinks the additional investment into your best ideas is likely to yield a better result than investment into your 20th or 30th favorite company.

2 b. Buffett is not scared by volatility. Rather, he does not invest in companies that are outside his circle of competence, which includes many technology companies.

3 a. A margin of safety is the difference between a stock's price and the company's underlying intrinsic value. Since no intrinsic value calculation is perfect, Buffett requires a satisfactory margin for error before he makes an investment.

4 c. Though the economics of a business are the most important factor, Buffett believes it's important to work with competent, honest managers. He believes that he has never made a good deal with a bad person.

5 a. Buffett focuses on the intrinsic value of businesses, not stock prices and the behavior of "Mr. Market."

Quiz 308: Know What You Own—Peter Lynch

1 b. Lynch managed the Fidelity Magellan fund from 1977 until 1990. When he retired, Fidelity Magellan had $13 billion in assets and an average total return of 25% per year.

2 b. Lynch invested in those in industries he understood. Lynch firmly believes that you should invest only in what you know. He shunned industries he didn't understand, even if they presented great value or great possibilities. Notice this echoes Warren Buffett's "circle of competence" idea.

3 c. Opportunistic. Lynch took ideas from many different investment philosophies. He went wherever he thought the best opportunities were.

4 a. Lynch looked for profitable companies with solid business models selling at good prices. He was willing to pay more for those companies than other managers might have paid, and he tolerated debt as long as the profits were there and the business model was right.

5 c. Lynch argues that the stock market is completely irrelevant. Moreover, he thinks that it is impossible to predict what stocks will do in the short term and recommends investing only for the long run.

Quiz 309: The Rest of the Hall of Fame

1 a. Bill Ruane (as well as Warren Buffett) studied under Ben Graham.

2 c. Bill Miller is distinctive among value investors because he is not afraid to own fast-growing companies.

3 a. All three investors listed won't pay a premium valuation for an investment, but Ralph Wanger is the one best known for buying small companies.

4 b. Bill Nygren has his own take on the 80/20 rule of thumb. He looks for stocks where 80% of the commentary about a company (presumably negative commentary) revolves around a piece of the company's business that contributes only about 20% of the profits.

5 c. All the investors in this chapter are focused on the price they are paying. Remember, even the best quality company may not be a good investment if you pay too much for its stock.

Quiz 310: Constructing a Portfolio

1   b.   Ninety percent of the benefits of diversification are achieved by holding 12 to 18 stocks.

2   b.   Unsystematic risk is the risk involved in holding individual companies. It can be diversified away by holding a larger number of stocks.

3   b.   If you hold a diversified portfolio, on average you should expect to achieve a market rate of return. By holding a concentrated portfolio, you increase your chances of obtaining a better return than the market, but at the same time, you also increase your risk of obtaining a lower rate of return than the market.

4   c.   Assuming that you are a good stock-picker, your returns should be better than the market some of the time. It would be rare to beat the market every year.

5   c.   If you hold too few stocks, you run the risk that one bad stock pick could produce an extremely large loss. For example, if you owned three stocks, each worth one-third of your portfolio, and one of your stocks went to zero, your portfolio would lose one-third of its value. Swinging only at fat pitches is good, not bad.

Quiz 311: Introduction to Options

1   a.   The intrinsic value of an option is the difference between the current stock price and the option's strike price, assuming the option is in the money.

2   b.   The call option is currently out of the money since the stock is trading below the strike price. Therefore, all of the option's value is time value.

3   c.   Theta measures the time value in an option. A theta of 0.25 means the option would lose $0.25 per day in time value, assuming no change in the underlying stock price. Remember that, all else equal, options tend to become less valuable over time.

4   a.   Each option contract covers the right to buy or sell 100 shares.

5   b.   Options can indeed create greater returns than stocks, but not without greater risk.

Quiz 312: Unconventional Equities

1 c. REITs and MLPs make consistent cash payments to equity holders, but cash flows from royalty trusts are much less predictable. Royalty trusts are affected by swings in production levels and commodity prices.

2 b. Answers A and C are only half true. MLP unitholders pay regular income tax annually on their share of the partnership's net income, which is almost always lower than cash distributed. The remaining portion of the cash distribution is treated as a return of capital and is taxed at the capital gains rate when the units are sold.

3 a. Royalty trust revenue comes from the production of resources like natural gas, oil, and coal; thus, the trust's revenue fluctuates as the price of the underlying commodity fluctuates.

4 c. Since MLP cash distributions are so steady, many investors treat them like bonds. Thus, when interest rates rise, bond and MLP prices tend to fall. This relationship is not perfect, but it generally holds over time.

5 b. Property taxes must be paid on real estate held in REITs, but these taxes are paid by the REIT and not the shareholders. Property taxes make up around 25% of most REITs' expenses.

Worksheet 301: The Fat-Pitch Strategy

1   The fat-pitch approach to investing is based on a baseball analogy. Instead of watching borderline pitches go by, batters often swing away because they fear being called out on strikes. Unlike these batters, investors following the fat-pitch approach will wait until they get the perfect pitch (investment opportunity) to swing at. We interpret this to mean that investors should patiently wait to buy until they find the stock of a wide-moat company that is trading at a sufficient margin of safety to its fair value estimate.

2   1.   Look for wide-moat companies.
       2.   Always have a margin of safety.
       3.   Don't be afraid to hold cash.
       4.   Don't be afraid to hold relatively few stocks.
       5.   Don't trade very often.

3   There are two closely related reasons why individual investors have advantages over professional money managers. First, professionals' performance is typically measured against the return of some sort of market benchmark, such as the S&P 500. Thus, these professionals are typically most concerned with outperforming their benchmark target—relative performance—rather than limiting their investments to only the very best opportunities.

Second, on a related note, many professionals are either required to, or feel the pressure to, be fully invested (or close to it) at all times. Thus, professionals are often investing in stocks that they'd prefer to pass on normally, just for the sake of staying fully invested. When the market drops, they're required to either sit and watch or sell some of their holdings for lower prices.

Individuals on the other hand can patiently hold on to cash until fat-pitch opportunities present themselves, and then they can buy boldly. Over the long term, this strategy has a very high probability of providing strong absolute returns, which should be more important to individuals than beating some sort of benchmark.

Worksheet 302: Psychology and Investing

1   An individual putting money toward savings while carrying a large credit card debt with a high
    interest penalty isn't optimizing the use of capital. We often think of money very discretely
    (i.e., this amount must go to savings, this amount must go to credit card debt, etc.) and we fail
    to see, for example, the penalty we pay by carrying a debt. More than likely, the wise move,
    in addition to reducing spending, would be to use some money from savings to pay down the debt.

2   We might use self-handicapping behaviors, such as saying, "It's a risky investment that could bomb,"
    so that we can save face should it not perform well. Such behavior may prompt us to accept risks
    that we shouldn't because we feel we've defended ourselves against a worst-case scenario.

3   It might be an indication of anchoring behavior, whereby we place too much emphasis on recent
    performance. Placing too much emphasis on what we know, and falling victim to representativeness,
    we might assume that utility stocks are also the best investment for the future, when that might
    not be the case. This behavior could also fall under the umbrella of herding.

4   Failing to look at something objectively, and instead favoring information that supports a pre-existing
    thesis, can lead to inaccurate and unfounded beliefs. We can become overconfident in our investing
    acumen, for example, because the only information we've acknowledged supports what we believed
    in the first place.

Worksheet 303: The Case for Dividends

1   Payout Ratio = Dividend Per Share ÷ Earnings Per Share
    For Peter's, the calculation reads: $1.40 ÷ $2.25 = 62%.

    Remember that the current payout ratio is only part of the story. You'll also have to consider whether
    or not earnings per share are sustainable, as well as the company's need to fund growth. Assuming
    a stable state, though, a 62% payout ratio should not be excessive.

2   Sustainable Growth = Return on Equity × (1 − Payout Ratio)
    For Peter's, the calculation reads: 14% × (1 − 0.62) = 5.3%.

    Assuming that the company has investment opportunities sufficient to grow the business at this rate,
    earnings and dividends should rise at 5.3% over the long term.

continued...

3   Required Retention Ratio (R3) = Expected Growth ÷ Return on Equity
     For Peter's, the calculation reads: 3% ÷ 14% = 21.4%.

     This tells us that, all else equal, it would take only 21.4% of earnings to fund 3% growth. Growth
     in excess of 5.3%—the sustainable growth rate calculated in question 2—would require the
     firm to retain more earnings (by cutting the dividend), issue additional stock (and dilute growth and
     returns on a per-share basis), or take measures to improve return on equity (reduce costs and/or
     increase leverage).

4   Cost of Growth = Required Retention Ratio × Earnings Per Share
     For Peter's, the calculation reads: 21.4% × $2.25 = $0.48

     In other words, Peter's Monster Trucks will need to retain $0.48 in per-share earnings to support a
     3% growth rate.

5   Excess Earnings Yield = (Earnings Per Share − Dividend Per Share − Cost of Growth) ÷ Stock Price
     For Peter's, the calculation reads: ($2.25 − $1.40 − $0.48) ÷ $36 = $0.37 ÷ $36 = 1.0%

     Since Peter's Monster Trucks is expanding at less than its sustainable growth rate, the company will
     earn $0.37 per share more than is needed to fund the dividend and the cost of growth. Remaining
     funds could be used for a number of purposes, but for the sake of conservatism, we assume the
     return will be equal to the company's current earnings yield.

6   Total Return = Dividend Yield + Expected Growth + (Excess Earnings ÷ Stock Price)
     For Peter's, the calculation reads: 3.9% + 3.0% + 1.0% = 7.9%

     With this final calculation we've obtained a prospective total return for the stock. This model makes
     several important assumptions—the sustainability of current earnings, a constant payout ratio,
     stable returns on equity, and long-term growth in perpetuity. Any of these factors could change. But
     if the business is mature and relatively consistent, 7.9% seems like a reasonable return to expect.

7   Compared with the stock market's historical returns of 10% or more, a 7.9% total return prospect
     doesn't sound too hot. However, one should also consider the risk profile of the business—if
     Peter's Monster Trucks is a very low-risk business, a 7.9% return might be acceptable. But make
     sure you're getting a margin of safety, of course!

Worksheet 304: 20 Stock-Investing Tips

1   If a piece of data is irrelevant to a company's future cash flow, it is probably not a good idea to anchor on it. Some examples include: the price you paid for a stock, your unrealized capital gains or losses on a stock, the trading volume of a stock, and a stock's past pricing history.

2   *"Going with the crowd is okay. If most people are buying something, they must know something I don't."* Wrong. Remember, think independently.

"The economics of a business do not matter as long as management is highly educated." Wrong. Business economics usually trump competence of management.

"Even a company with an attractive business should be avoided if snakes are in charge." Right. If a company's management is more interested in lining their own pockets than increasing value for shareholders, watch out.

"Past performance of management should never be considered because it is of no relevance to future performance." Wrong. Past performance is no guarantee of future results, but it is still a good indicator.

"You don't need a margin of safety if you are buying a company with a wide moat and excellent management." Wrong. You should always require a margin of safety in your stock investments. Higher-quality companies, such as those with a wide economic moat, can be bought with a smaller margin of safety than those of riskier, less attractive firms.

"Fear and greed can negatively impact your investment decision making." Right. Often the best time to buy is when everyone else is fearful because prices have just dropped. Likewise, often the time to sell is when others are greedy because prices have just risen.

"It is a good thing when company management has a significant ownership stake in the firm they are running." Right. If managers don't own stock in their companies, they may not have their interests aligned with those of shareholders.

"Quality companies can be purchased at any price." Wrong. Remember, the difference between a great company and a great investment is the price you pay.

Worksheet 305: Deep Value—Benjamin Graham

1   Graham's intrinsic value formula is as follows:

Value = Current (Normal) Earnings × (8.5 + Twice the Expected Annual Growth Rate)

By plugging in our numbers we get:

Value = $1 × (8.5 + (2 × 5))
Value = $1 × (18.5)
Value = $18.50

Erika's Bookstores' estimated intrinsic value is $18.50. With the stock currently trading at $12.50, it appears to be undervalued and would warrant further investigation.

2   We would need additional information about Erika's, such as details about its competitive advantages and risk to accurately gauge an appropriate margin of safety. However, with a current market price that is 67.5% of the intrinsic value calculated from Graham's formula, the company is a good candidate for further research.

3   By rearranging Graham's formula, we can calculate the growth expectations embedded in a stock's price.

Expected Growth = (P/E Ratio − 8.5) × 1/2

Once again, we plug in our numbers:

P/E Ratio = $32 ÷ $0.38 = 84.2
Expected Growth = (84.2 − 8.5) × 1/2
Expected Growth = 37.9%

At $32 per share, the market is expecting Peter Trading to grow earnings per share by 37.9% annually for the next 10 years.

Worksheet 306: Holding Superior Growth— Philip Fisher

1   There is no exact answer here, but your sentence should read something like this: Purchase and hold for the long term a concentrated portfolio of outstanding companies with compelling growth prospects that you understand very well.

continued…

2   According to one of Fisher's 15 points, a company must have a worthwhile profit margin. All other things being equal, the company with $500 million in sales is more attractive because its annual profit is $50 million, while the company with $1 billion in sales earned only $10 million.

3   Company has a new product with the potential to reach $500 million in sales in five years:
Research Further

Company's research-and-development efforts have consistently failed to produce products with sizable sales and profit potential:
Avoid

Company has a sales organization that is recognized to be one of the best in the industry:
Research Further

Company's management is obsessed with meeting Wall Street's quarterly profit estimates:
Avoid

Company has grown 100% over the past three years, funded by issuing 50% more shares:
Avoid

Company's management is as equally candid about failures as it is about successes:
Research Further

Worksheet 307: Great Companies at Reasonable Prices—Warren Buffett

1   The margin of safety is $10. It is the estimated fair value of the stock minus the market price at the time of purchase: $50 − $40 = $10.

2   No, you should not be guided by the market price. Rather, you should be guided by your diligent calculations of the company's fair value. If the fair value estimate remains at $20, then you might consider an additional purchase, because $10 is an even more attractive price than the initial purchase price of $15. The price drop would certainly not be a reason to sell unless the fundamentals guiding the original fair value estimate have deteriorated.

3   Berkshire Hathaway's home page and its annual reports are very simple and not flashy at all. The annual reports to shareholders are worth the time to read.

Worksheet 308: Know What You Own— Peter Lynch

1   There is no right or wrong answer here. The point is to train yourself to look around for promising businesses in your everyday life. While not all candidates will be worthwhile (or even publicly traded), you may uncover some hidden gems that merit further research before Wall Street finds them. Recall Lynch's success with the L'eggs pantyhose sold by Hanes.

2   The Lynch investment philosophy has four main components:
1) Invest only in what you understand.
2) Do your homework and research the company thoroughly.
3) Focus only on the company's fundamentals and not the market as a whole.
4) Invest only for the long run and discard short-term market gyrations.

3   The answer to this question will depend on your understanding of doughnuts and semiconductors. Based on Lynch's stock-picking approach, you should invest only in what you know. Therefore, if you understand doughnuts but not semiconductors, you should invest in doughnuts (assuming you can find an attractive doughnut company). Alternatively, if you have a solid grasp on semiconductors but not doughnuts, you should invest in semiconductors.

4   Company has pension liabilities that far exceed its pension assets:
Avoid

Company has earnings growth rate that is triple its P/E ratio:
Research Further

Company's insiders are buying the stock:
Research Further

Company is in a fast-growth industry Lynch knows little about:
Avoid

Company is on the cover of several large magazines:
Avoid

Company spends a lot of money every year on acquisitions in various industries:
Avoid

Company is touted on television as "the next Microsoft":
Avoid

Company creates simple, widely recognized but low-growth product:
Research Further

Worksheet 309: The Rest of the Hall of Fame

1   Write down the name of the great investor most likely to be associated with the following:

A. Reading a history book: **Munger.**
B. Buying a company that has a major short-term issue: **Whitman.**
C. Making a single company 25% of his portfolio: **Ruane.**
   (Bill Miller is also known to have highly concentrated positions.)
D. Buying a stock that has no Wall Street analysts covering it: **Wanger.**
E. Hanging out with Warren Buffett: **Munger.**
F. Buying a three-year-old company that is growing fast: **Miller.**
G. Avoiding a stock because he doesn't trust a company's management: **Nygren.**
   (To be fair, this would be an issue for nearly every investor mentioned in this chapter.)
H. Seeing a trend and acting on an investment theme: **Wanger.**

2   There are actually four common threads.
   1. All are willing to challenge conventional wisdom.
   2. All invest for the long term—meaning, none are day-trading.
   3. All look for solid companies.
   4. All are very aware of the price they are paying for their investments.

3   With worldly wisdom, investors can stay focused on what matters while others are running for the doors due to a short-term blip. In other words, the worldly wisdom Munger preaches can help savvy investors profit from others' shortsightedness.

4   Clearly, there is a world of investing wisdom to be had for free if one knows where to look.

Worksheet 310: Constructing a Portfolio

1   Technically speaking, holding 20 stocks in her portfolio does not mean that Christine is properly diversified. Her stocks are in only two sectors of the stock market, and therefore her returns are probably highly correlated to what happens in those two sectors. However, Christine's circle of competence is in finance and consumer stocks, which increases her ability to make money from her investments in those sectors. She could also consider a good mutual fund to get exposure to areas outside her circle of competence.

continued...

2   There are no right answers. However, one way of looking at Ron's portfolio is to notice that he really owns 10 stocks directly and another 340 stocks indirectly through his four mutual funds (large-blend mutual funds normally hold about 85 stocks each). Therefore, Ron owns 350 stocks, with about 5% of his wealth invested in each of his 10 largest stock holdings. If he is comfortable with having 50% of his equity in 10 great companies, then we believe his overall portfolio is diversified.

3   Here are a few of Maria's options:

a. Purchase U.S. stocks that have extensive international operations.
b. Purchase international stocks that have U.S. listings.
c. Purchase international stocks on a foreign exchange.
d. Own an international equity mutual fund.

Ultimately, Maria's choice would depend on her circle of competence and comfort level. While Maria may feel comfortable with picking her own stocks, she may not feel competent selecting stocks internationally.

Worksheet 311: Introduction to Options

1   You could sell puts with a strike price of $45. If the stock fell below $45, the person who bought the puts will likely exercise his or her option, and you will have to buy the stock for $45.

2   Because you expect the stock will be worth more and it will become more valuable in the future, you may want to purchase calls with long time horizons, also known as leaps.

3   This is the notation for the call options expiring in March 2007 with a strike price of $75. Put another way, if you purchase these call options, you have the right to buy the stock for $75 anytime before the options expire in March 2007.

4   $7,500. Each contract covers 100 shares, so 10 contracts would give you the right to purchase 1,000 shares of stock (10 $\times$ 100). $7.50 $\times$ 100 $\times$ 10 = $7,500.

Worksheet 312: Unconventional Equities

1   An MLP unitholder pays regular taxes only on his or her portion of net income.

$0.35 \times 25\% \times 1,000 = \$87.50$

Total distributions $= 1,000 \times \$1.25 = \$1,250$.

2   Mike will recognize two sources of capital gains: market price appreciation and return of capital through cash distributions. Return of capital is simply distributions ($9.30) minus net income ($2.30), or $7.

Cost basis per share: $35 − \$7 = \$28$
Capital gains per share: $40 − \$28 = \$12$
Capital gains tax: $12 \times 15\% \times 600$ shares $= \$1,080$

3   Boston Properties specializes in office properties, with a geographical focus in Boston, Washington, D.C., Midtown Manhattan, and San Francisco. Dividends in the past five years were $2.04 per share in 2000, $2.27 in 2001, $2.41 in 2002, $2.50 in 2003, and $2.58 in 2004. Lease expirations after 2014 comprise 27.5% of all leases.

continued…

4   Arthur should choose the royalty trust, which would result in a net cash inflow of $765. Note that if we expected the prices of the investments to change during the year (and they most likely would in the real world), we would have additional gains/losses and tax effects to consider.

REIT

Dividend =	$6.40
Less: income tax = $4.00 × 30% =	-$1.20
Less: capital gains tax = $2.40 × 15% =	-$0.36
Aftertax cash flows per share =	$4.84
Multiplied by: # of units owned	125.00
Aftertax income =	$605.00

MLP

Cash distribution =	$3.50
Less: income tax = $1.50 × 30% =	-$0.45
Less: capital gains tax =($3.50 − $1.50) × 15% =	-$0.30
Aftertax cash flows per unit =	$2.75
Multiplied by: # of units owned	200.00
Aftertax income =	$550.00

Royalty Trust

Cash distribution =	$3.60
Less: capital gains tax = $3.60 × 15% =	-$0.54
Aftertax cash flows per unit =	$3.06
Multiplied by: # of units owned	250.00
Aftertax income =	$765.00

Investing Terms

10-K

The statutory annual report of a company's activities that is filed with the Securities and Exchange Commission. The 10-K tends to be the most comprehensive of a company's periodic filings. Note that these reports contain audited financial statements, whereas the statements within quarterly reports (10-Qs) are not audited.

10-Q

The statutory quarterly report of a company's activities that is filed with the Securities and Exchange Commission. The 10-Q tends to be less comprehensive than the annual (10-K) filing but provides useful short-term information and changes within the company. Note that the financial statements contained in a quarterly report are unaudited, unlike those in annual (10-K) reports.

20-F

Annual report submitted to the Securities and Exchange Commission by foreign companies that are publicly traded on a U.S. exchange. The 20-F is similar to the 10-K submitted by U.S. companies.

401(k)

A regulated defined-contribution retirement account set up by companies for their employees. The name comes from the IRS code that governs the plans.

Participants in 401(k)s are allowed to direct a portion of their pretax income into accounts that are allowed to grow tax-free. Distributions are taxed (at a presumably lower tax rate in retirement), and early distributions before retirement age are generally penalized.

40-F

The annual report filed with the Securities and Exchange Commission by Canadian companies that are publicly traded on a U.S. exchange. The 40-F is similar to the 10-K report that U.S. companies must file.

A

Accounts Payable

An accounting entry on the liabilities side of the balance sheet that typically represents what companies owe to their vendors.

Accounts Receivable

An accounting entry on the asset side of the balance sheet that typically represents bills outstanding for services already rendered. One company's accounts receivable is usually another company's accounts payable.

Accrual Accounting

A method of accounting in which revenue is recorded when earned and expenses are recorded when incurred. This recognition of earnings and expenses may not correspond to when cash is actually received or spent. Publicly traded companies in the United States use accrual accounting.

American Depository Receipt (ADR)

A certificate issued by a bank that represents a set number of shares in a foreign corporation. ADRs make it easier for Americans to invest in foreign companies. They are traded on an exchange like stocks, which allows for liquidity and current price information.

American Stock Exchange (AMEX)

One of a number of U.S. stock exchanges where investors can trade shares of certain companies.

Amortization

1. The gradual, systematic elimination of a liability.

2. A noncash expense that represents the decline of an intangible asset's value over time.

Analyst Upgrades/Downgrades

A revision in a Wall Street analyst's rating, such as "Buy," "Hold," or "Sell," for a particular stock. When a stock's rating is upgraded or downgraded, the stock price will often move in that direction.

Anchoring

A behavioral finance term used to describe investors' tendency to place undue emphasis on recent performance or an irrelevant data point, such as the purchase price of a stock.

Annual Report

A report provided by a company to its shareholders that includes information on the company's activities in the past fiscal year. The term "annual report" may refer to the 10-K filed with the SEC or the less comprehensive glossy report distributed by a company that may have only a portion of the information contained in the 10-K.

Annual Shareholder Meeting

The annual gathering of shareholders of public firms to review new company developments and vote on any outstanding matters.

Annuity

A financial instrument that makes fixed payments over a predetermined number of periods.

Asset

Any item that a company may own. Assets include cash, property, buildings, machinery, and so on.

Asset Class

A category of investments with similar characteristics. Some of the most common asset classes include stocks, bonds, mutual funds, real estate, bank accounts, and cash.

Asset/Equity Ratio

Total assets divided by total shareholders' equity. The asset/equity ratio (also known as the equity multiplier) is indicative of a company's liquidity and stability. Generally, a high asset/equity ratio is worthy of concern but should be viewed within the context of a company's industry peers.

Asset Turnover Ratio

A measure of how many dollars in revenue a company has generated per each dollar of assets, calculated as sales divided by total assets. Generally, the higher this ratio, the more efficient the company.

B

Baby Put

A put option that is far out of the money with a subsequently small price.

Balance Sheet

A financial statement that shows what a company owns (its assets), what it owes (its liabilities), and the difference between the two (its equity). The balance sheet, one of the three main financial statements, is a snapshot of a company's financial health at a specific point in time such as the end of the year.

Barrier to Entry

A hypothetical obstruction to competition such as brand strength, economies of scale, patents, and copyrights that protect the profits of a company. *See Economic Moat.*

Basic Shares

The number of shares of stock that a company has outstanding. This is often compared with the diluted share count, which accounts for the effects of shares that could be issued via options and convertible bonds.

Basis

The purchase price of a capital asset such as stocks or bonds. Basis (also known as cost basis) is important in computing potential capital gains taxes.

Behavioral Finance

The study of how human psychology affects financial decision-making.

Beta

A statistical measure of the volatility of a given stock relative to the volatility of the overall market. *See Volatility.*

Bid/Ask Spread

The difference between the highest price someone in the market is willing to pay for a stock (the bidding price) and the lowest price for which someone is willing to sell a stock (the asking price). In general, the larger the market for a given stock, the lower the spread will be. The bid/ask spread is one of the frictional costs of trading.

Board of Directors

A collection of individuals elected by shareholders to steer a company in the most profitable direction. In most situations, company executives (CEO, CFO, etc.) report to the board of directors. Executives are hired, fired, and directed by their boards, not shareholders directly.

Bond

A loan made to a company or government for a certain amount of time (the bond's term or maturity) typically in return for regular interest payments, otherwise known as coupons. Bonds are the primary way companies raise debt capital to finance their operations.

Book Value

1. The value of an asset on the balance sheet calculated as historical cost less accumulated depreciation.

2. The theoretical value of a company if it were immediately liquidated today, calculated as total assets minus liabilities, intangible assets, and preferred stock. Book value is represented on the balance sheet as common equity. Value investors often start their research for undervalued companies with those that are trading at or below their book value.

Buffett, Warren

Chairman and CEO of Berkshire Hathaway and renowned value investor. Also known as the "Oracle of Omaha," Warren Buffett is considered by some to be the greatest investor of our generation and by others to be the greatest investor of all time. He is most often associated with value investing, where intrinsic value is paramount. Buffett's stellar investing record is often used to show that the market is not perfectly efficient and that high-level statistics are not necessary to become an outstanding investor.

Buyer Power

The negotiating strength of a product's purchaser. Strong buyers put pressure on sellers to decrease prices while maintaining or increasing quality. Buyer power is an important component to Michael Porter's Five Forces Model.

Bylaws

Rules governing management established by a company when incorporated.

C

Call

An option represented by a contract that allows the purchaser to buy a stock from a second party at a given price within a certain amount of time. The other party, or "writer of the call," is obligated to provide the stock and is compensated for this risk by a premium—the price of the contract. The call holder will exercise the option only when the strike price of the call is less than the current market price. The difference between these two numbers, less the premium paid, is the call holder's gain.

Capital

The cash or other resources that a company uses to make money. Generally, a company tries to achieve the greatest income with as little capital as possible. There are two types of capital—debt capital (provided by lenders) and equity capital (provided by owners). When a company sells stock in itself, it is raising equity capital.

Capital Asset Pricing Model (CAPM)

An efficient market theory convention that calculates the value of a stock as the risk-free rate plus that stock's beta (*see Volatility*) times the market premium.

Capital Gain/Loss

Gain or loss realized when an asset, such as a stock or bond, is sold for more or less than its basis, or original purchase price.

Cash Accounting

Method of accounting in which revenue is recorded when cash is received, and expenses are recorded when cash is spent. This can be contrasted with accrual accounting.

Cash Flow Statement

See Statement of Cash Flows.

Cash Flow to the Firm

One of the methods of valuing a company via a discounted cash-flow analysis. This measures cash flow independent of the capital structure.

Charter

A filing that describes the basic purposes of a proposed company. The charter is also known as the articles of incorporation.

Circle of Competence

The area of one's investing aptitude. Investors often fare best when they stay within their circle of competence when selecting investments—in other words, "stick to what you know."

Cognitive Dissonance

A psychological term used to describe the inability to hold two seemingly disparate ideas, opinions, beliefs, attitudes, or behaviors at once.

Commissions

The fees paid to brokers and financial advisors for the services they provide, including executing trades. Any profit-maximizing investor should seek to minimize commissions paid.

Compensation Committee

A group usually composed of company insiders and board members that determines appropriate executive incentives, which generally consist of salary, bonuses, and stock options.

Competitive Position

The ability of one company to outperform another company based on a variety of attributes. *See Economic Moat.*

Compound Interest

Interest that accrues on top of interest, or gains that beget more gains. To calculate the future value of an investment, you need to know the investment amount, the rate of return (or interest rate), and the number of periods the investment will be allowed to compound.

Confirmation Bias

A psychological term describing how people treat information that supports what is already believed, or desired, more favorably.

Contract

An agreement between the writer and the buyer of an option to either buy or sell a stock at a given price. This agreement gives the purchaser the "option" to purchase (or sell) the security, while requiring the writer of the contract to sell (or buy) if the option holder so chooses.

Corporate Governance

Internal and external controls that promote and maintain fair business practices. *See Stewardship.*

Cost of Capital

The expenses a company incurs from the use of debt or equity, usually expressed as a percentage. The weighted average cost of capital combines the cost of equity and the cost of debt into a single rate used to discount cash flows when valuing a company using the cash flow to the firm method.

Cost of Debt

The return investors in a company's debt receive in exchange for taking on risk. The cost of debt is determined by the credit quality of a firm. The riskier the firm, the higher its cost of debt.

Cost of Equity

The return equity investors expect to receive on their investment for the risk they are assuming when becoming an owner. A company's cost of equity is less tangible than its cost of debt. In general, a riskier company will have a higher cost of equity.

Cost of Goods Sold (COGS)

Expenses, such as for raw materials or labor, found on the income statement that are directly related to the goods or services provided by a company. For many companies, COGS (also known as "cost of sales") is the largest expense incurred and is therefore important in determining profitability.

Creditor

The person or institution, such as a bank, that loans money to a borrower in exchange for interest and the eventual return of principal. Creditors provide debt capital to companies.

Cyclicals

The stocks of companies whose prosperity tends to be heavily dependent on economic growth. Cyclicals tend to be capital-intensive businesses, such as auto and steel makers, that perform extremely well when economic growth is strong, but struggle, sometimes severely, when growth is weak or recessionary.

D

Day Trading

The act of quickly trading in and out of stocks in an often futile attempt to accumulate a large quantity of small gains caused by intraday fluctuations in stock prices. Those who trade excessively work against the tide in terms of both taxes and commissions.

Deferred Revenue

An accounting liability created by accrual accounting when a company collects cash ahead of when it recognizes revenue. The cash is already in the door, but the liability is the promise of future goods or services.

Degree of Rivalry

A component of Michael Porter's Five Forces Model that indicates the intensity of competition in an industry. The higher the degree of rivalry, the more difficult it is for firms to raise prices and maintain profitability.

Depreciation

A noncash expense that represents an asset's normal wear and tear. Depreciation reduces the book value of the asset.

Deworsifiers

Peter Lynch's parody of diversifiers. Lynch argued that investors or companies who overstressed the importance of diversification often "deworsified" their performance by diluting their good ideas just to achieve variety.

Diluted Shares

The total number of shares a company would have outstanding if all potentially convertible securities, such as options or convertible bonds, were converted into shares (i.e., basic shares plus converted shares).

Discount Factor

In a discounted cash-flow analysis, the number that combines the discount rate and the number of periods a cash flow is to be discounted. For example, given a 10% discount rate and five periods, the discount factor is $1/(1+0.10)^5 = 0.62$.

Discount Rate

The rate at which a future cash flow is discounted to determine its present value. The weighted average cost of capital is a common example.

Discounted Cash Flow (DCF)

The present value of a future cash flow, or flows. In the discounted cash-flow model of valuation, the sum of all future cash flows is an estimate of a company's present value. Discounting is necessary to account for the opportunity costs incurred through the passage of time—"a dollar today is worth more than a dollar tomorrow."

Distribution
An amount of money, similar to a dividend, that is paid to the partners of a master limited partnership according to their percentage ownership. For tax purposes, distributions usually have a large portion that is considered a return of capital rather than income.

Dividend
Cash distributed by companies to their shareholders. Dividends may occur quarterly, yearly, or on special occasions. Older, more established companies tend to pay out a large percentage of their profits, while newer, growth-oriented companies tend to pay low dividends or none at all. Dividends can also be distributed as stock, but this practice is not common.

Dividend Rate
The amount of dividends paid expressed as a percentage of earnings or more, often as an absolute dollar amount.

Dividend Reinvestment Plan (DRIP)
An optional plan offered by some corporations that allows immediate reinvestment of dividends into additional shares, sometimes at a discount to the current market price. DRIPs can be an effective method of investing for those who don't need current income.

Dividend Yield
The dividends per share of a company over the trailing one-year period as a percentage of the current stock price. Dividend yield is often compared with the current yield of bonds, which is a bond's coupon divided by the bond's price.

Dollar Cost Averaging
A systematic, periodic investment of a fixed dollar amount. When investment prices fall, a greater amount of the investment (i.e., more shares) are purchased, and vice versa.

Dow Jones Industrial Average (DJIA)
An index of 30 large companies representing several industries. The DJIA (or "The Dow" for short) was first published in 1896 and is frequently used as a gauge of the overall stock market.

DuPont Equation
An equation that allows for in-depth analysis of a firm's return on assets (ROA) and return on equity (ROE). The DuPont equation provides information on a firm's profitability, asset utilization, and financial leverage. This increased breakdown of ROA and ROE inputs allows for a better understanding of a company's internal workings.

E

Earnings Per Share (EPS)
The amount of net income a company earned divided by the number of shares outstanding. For example, if a firm earned $1 million last year and had 100,000 shares of stock outstanding, its EPS would have been $10 for the year ($1 million/100,000 shares = $10).

Earnings Surprise
The difference between a company's actual financial results for a given period and what Wall Street analysts expected. Usually there is a share price increase for positive earnings surprises and a price decrease for negative earnings surprises, depending on the magnitude of the discrepancy.

Earnings Yield
The inverse of the P/E (price/earnings) ratio. For example, if the current price of a stock is $20, last year's earnings were $1 million, and there are 4 million shares outstanding, then the earnings per share is $0.25 ($1 million/4 million shares = $0.25), and the earnings yield is 1.25% ($0.25/$20 = 0.0125, 1.25%).

EBITDA
A financial metric representing earnings before interest, taxes, depreciation, and amortization. EBITDA can be a useful proxy for a company's gross cash flow.

Economic Moat
A framework used to measure a company's ability to maintain a competitive advantage for an extended period. (The term "economic moat" is derived from a phrase originally coined by Warren Buffett.) Think of a great company (and its profits) as a castle surrounded by a wide moat that attackers (competitors) would have an extremely difficult time crossing. Contrast this with a not-so-great, no-moat company whose competitors can attack with ease. The width of an economic moat (strength of competitive advantages) is crucial in determining how profitable a company is, and how long it can maintain this status. Common sources of economic moats include being the low-cost producer, benefiting from switching costs, having a network effect, and holding intangible assets such as patents, copyrights, and brands.

Economies of Scale
A desirable situation in which the cost per unit of production decreases as output increases. This occurs because of operating efficiencies usually caused by large fixed cost outlays for mass-production machinery, a large enough labor force to allow for specialization, or the ability to buy supplies in bulk for a lower price than competitors pay. Economies of scale can lead to a sizable economic moat that protects a company's profitability.

Enterprise Value

Calculated by adding a company's market capitalization to its debt minus cash. Enterprise value is a useful approximation for the "buyout value" of a company.

Equity Capital

The capital contributed by a company's shareholders. Its value can be found from the balance sheet by summing the additional paid-in capital and common stock accounts. Equity capital may also be used in reference to shareholders' equity, in which case it is calculated as assets minus liabilities. In other words, equity is the difference between the value of what a company owns and what it owes. In general, a company with greater equity capital than debt capital is considered more stable.

Excess Cash

1. *See Free Cash Flow.*

2. Cash held by a company not needed to operate its business.

Exchange-Traded Fund (ETF)

A stock-like security that is structured to mimic an index. ETFs are similar to index funds offered by mutual fund companies except that they trade on an exchange, which gives investors the ability to sell short, buy on margin, and engage in any other activity normally associated with a stock.

Ex-Dividend Date

The date on which you must be holding a stock to receive an upcoming dividend.

Exercise

The act of realizing the intrinsic value of an option that is in the money. When exercising a call option, this is accomplished by buying a stock at below market prices, and when exercising a put option, this is accomplished by selling a stock at above market prices.

Expenses

The costs of doing business such as labor, materials, and taxes.

Expiration

The date when an option contract becomes worthless. This occurs when the price of a stock did not rise above (as was expected by the holder of a call) or fall below (as was expected by the holder of a put) the strike price.

F

Fair Value Estimate

An estimate of a stock's intrinsic worth today. In a discounted cash-flow model, the fair value estimate is calculated by summing up the value of all future cash flows in terms of today's dollars.

Fat Pitch

An approach to investing that hinges on patience and quality over quantity. The name is derived from a baseball analogy—since there are no called strikes in investing, it can be advantageous to wait for a fat pitch (an excellent company selling at a reasonable price), then swing for the fences.

Fee-Based Planner

A financial planner who provides research and suggestions regarding the allocation of an investor's funds for a fixed fee (as opposed to trading commissions). It is important to be aware of a planner's incentives to ensure that you share the same goals.

Fidelity Magellan

The mutual fund managed by Peter Lynch from 1977 to 1990 that enjoyed well-above-average returns during his tenure.

Fiduciary Duty

The responsibility an executive has to act on behalf of a company and its shareholders in regard to financial matters.

Fisher, Philip

A successful investor and author best known for the book *Common Stocks and Uncommon Profits*. He achieved success through diligent research and a long-term mentality.

Five Forces Model

A framework developed by Harvard professor Michael Porter used to describe the external pressures a company faces. It consists of buyer and supplier bargaining power, the threat of new entrants and substitutes, and the intensity of rivalry among industry competitors.

Form 4

A statutory filing required by the SEC to disclose stock transactions by a shareholder owning 10% or more of a company's outstanding shares. These can be telling of significant stockholders' opinions about the stock they own.

Forward Price/Earnings (Forward P/E)

Next year's earnings divided by the current market price of a stock.

Framing Effect

A behavioral finance term used to describe how the use of a reference point can affect decisions.

Free Cash Flow

The cash a company generated from its core business operations minus the expenses incurred to keep the company running. Free cash flow is called "free" because it represents the amount of money that a company's management is free to pay out to shareholders or use to fund new opportunities without harming the existing business. It is calculated from the statement of cash flows by taking net cash provided by operating activities minus capital expenditures, which are listed in the cash flows from investing activities, also on the cash flow statement.

Free Cash Flow to Equity

One of two primary methods of discounted cash-flow analysis. This method measures free cash flows and discounts them by the cost of equity.

Full-Service Broker

A more expensive alternative to a discount broker that provides research and suggestions regarding the allocation of an investor's funds.

Fundamental Equity Risk Premium

The return above the risk-free rate required by investors for a given stock, usually calculated by taking into consideration "fundamental" risk factors such as cyclicality, the predictability of cash flow, and even management quality. The riskier the investment, the greater the required premium.

Funds from Operations (FFO)

The cash flow from a REIT's operations, similar to the earnings per share of a stock. FFO is calculated as earnings plus the noncash expenses of depreciation and amortization.

Future Value

The value of a cash flow today projected into the future, taking into account the effects of compounding.

G

General Partner

The company, public or private, that is responsible for the operations of a master limited partnership.

Graham, Benjamin

Author best known for *The Intelligent Investor*—a book regarded by many as the bible of value investing. Graham was also Warren Buffett's most influential mentor.

Gross Profit

Revenues minus the cost of goods sold (COGS). Gross profit is one of many measures of profitability.

H

Herding Behavior

A psychology term used to describe how investors will follow a stock tip or the advice of others under the assumption that others have more information than they do.

Hindsight Bias

The tendency to re-evaluate our past behavior surrounding an event or decision after knowing the actual outcome.

House Money

A behavioral finance term referring to the notion that certain money, depending on how it was made, is less or more valuable than other money. For example, people will commonly take more risk with house money that was won, as it is often considered less real or valuable than earned income.

I

In the Money

A term used to refer to a call option whose strike price is below the current market price, or a put option whose strike price is above the current market price. The larger these differences, the "deeper" in the money the option becomes, and the more profitable the position.

Income Statement

A financial statement showing the money a firm has brought in (its revenues), the amount of money it has spent (its expenses), and the difference between the two (its profit). The income statement, one of the three main financial statements, covers a company's performance over a specific time period such as three months or one year and answers the question, "How much did the company make?"

Individual Retirement Account (IRA)

A type of investment account that gives its owners certain tax benefits. IRAS come in two flavors— "traditional" and "Roth." The common trait between the two types is that income in the accounts is allowed to grow tax-free.

Inflation

The upward movement in the prices of goods over time. Currencies tend to lose their value, or purchasing power, over time. This is important to consider when making an investment. Although this number can vary tremendously, the target rate in the U.S. is about 3%.

Initial Public Offering (IPO)

The act of selling a portion of a company to the general public by making shares of stock available on a stock exchange. "Going public" often raises millions, or even billions, of dollars in new capital for the company to invest in its operations.

Insider Transaction

A stock transaction conducted by a person possessing important nonpublic information about a company, such as an upcoming merger, divestiture, or any other material event. These transactions are unfair to other investors and, therefore, illegal.

Intangible Asset

An asset without a physical presence, such as intellectual property, a government approval, a brand name, a unique company culture, or a geographic advantage. Because they are difficult to quantify, intangible assets are sometimes excluded from certain valuation techniques and ratios. *See Economic Moat.*

Interest

The price paid for borrowed funds, or received for loaned funds. In an investment, such as a bond, the investor is loaning money to a corporation and in return receives interest on the principal loaned. Simple interest is paid off as accrued, and compound interest accumulates on itself, resulting in interest on top of interest.

Interest Expense

The cost of borrowing recognized on a corporation's income statement. As companies borrow more, interest expense becomes more burdensome. In a downturn, this fixed cost can cause bankruptcy in extreme cases. A good measure of a company's ability to pay its interest expense is the interest coverage ratio, which is operating profits divided by interest expense. The greater this multiple, the better.

Interest Income

Income from securities held by a company often in the form of corporate debt and money market accounts.

Interest Shield

The use of debt capital, the interest on which is typically tax-deductible, in order to "shield" earnings from taxes.

Intrinsic Value

1. The underlying value of a company not necessarily reflected on any financial statement. It can be thought of as the value of the firm today plus all of its potential value expected to result from future growth.

2. The potential gain realized by exercising an option. It is the difference between the strike price of the option and the current market price of the underlying stock.

Intrinsic Value Approach

A long-term investing philosophy that focuses on the value added by a company over an extended period. An investor following this approach must be capable of patiently waiting out short-term fluctuations with the belief that eventually a company's underlying value will be realized.

Inventory

An asset on the balance sheet that represents the finished, in-process, or raw goods a company intends to sell. Normally, inventory is considered a liquid asset that is regularly converted into cash.

Invested Capital

Funds allocated to a particular investment. For example, shareholders invest capital (cash) in stocks expecting a good return on this capital. Within a company, capital is invested in machinery, buildings, and any other asset needed to grow the business. Return on invested capital is a very important metric when considering a company.

L

Leverage

1. The percentage of a company's costs that are fixed, calculated as fixed costs divided by fixed plus variable costs, and referred to as operating leverage. High operating leverage increases risk by making the company less flexible in economic downturns. However, when the business is doing well, high operating leverage allows profits to increase very quickly once fixed costs are met.

2. The amount of debt versus equity used to finance a company's operations. High debt versus equity increases profit potential, but the fixed payments associated with large amounts of borrowed capital can be a significant burden when a business is struggling.

Liability

A debt, such as a loan or principal on bonds, owed by a company, usually to banks or to investors. Total liabilities, a line item on the balance sheet, can be a revealing metric in determining the financial health of a company. Liabilities can be calculated as a company's assets minus its equity.

Limit Order

A type of order placed with a broker for a stock transaction. The transaction is executed only if a stock trades below the named maximum buy price, or above the named minimum sell price.

Limited Partner

The public unitholders of a master limited partnership. Limited partners have limited control of the company, but their personal liability is also limited to their investment.

Long-Term Equity Anticipation Securities (LEAPS)

An option contract that has a long duration until expiration. This can be a safer method of predicting stock movement than traditional, shorter duration options because the additional time allows for greater price movement and less of a reliance on proper short-term timing. However, this added benefit is accompanied by a price tag that is often quite high.

Loss Aversion

A behavioral finance term used to describe the tendency to avoid selling declining stocks because of the unwillingness to accept defeat and admit a mistake.

Low-Cost Producer

A company that can deliver its goods or services at a lower cost than competitors can. Common ways to achieve this position are economies of scale and technology. This is one way for a company to form an economic moat.

Lynch, Peter

Managed the Fidelity Magellan Fund to well-above-average returns from 1977 to 1990 in addition to writing several revered investment books. Most of his success came from investing in companies early in their growth phase and staying within his circle of competence. He was a proponent of being aware of changes in your surroundings for signs of investment opportunities.

M

Margin

1. Total sales minus certain expenses, divided by total sales, expressed as a percentage. For example, the gross margin is the percentage of revenues that results in profit after costs of goods sold (COGS) have been subtracted.

2. A type of investment account in which the owner borrows against the value of the account.

Margin Call

Contact from a broker that a margin investment account has inadequate funds available. Investors using margin must maintain a certain portion of the account's value (often 50%) as equity with the other half being debt. If the equity's value falls below the required margin, which can occur when an account's value drops, then a margin call is made. Investors then have to put up more funds to boost the equity, or the broker will subsequently sell the investments held as collateral.

Margin of Safety

The discount an investor requires to a stock's fair value estimate before purchase to account for the uncertainties involved in valuing an investment. Smart investors require a margin of safety to account for the fact that their predictions may be wrong.

Market Capitalization

A company's total market price, calculated by multiplying the number of shares outstanding by the current price per share. This figure is often used when referring to the size of a company.

Market Order

A method of buying stock at the current market price. Generally, a market order gives a broker the go-ahead to purchase a security as soon as possible at the prevailing price.

Market Value

The most recent price quoted for a stock on an exchange.

Master Limited Partnership (MLP)

A publicly traded limited partnership. Similar to REITs, MLPs are exempt from corporate income taxes and pay out most of their cash flow in the form of distributions.

Maturity

The end of an investment period, most often applied to the date principal is returned in a bond investment.

Mental Accounting

The act of putting money into specific "buckets" for specific purposes.

Miller, Bill

Successful value investor with Legg Mason Funds who has consistently outperformed the market by buying stocks that typically do not fit the "value" mold.

Moat

See Economic Moat.

Modern Portfolio Theory

A statistical approach to portfolio management developed in the 1950s that tries to match a given risk tolerance (or aversion) with an optimal reward.

Monopoly

A situation where one company controls substantially all of a particular market. This can be achieved through the possession of a superior product, a patent, regulation, or, in unfortunate cases, by unsavory or even illegal business practices.

Mr. Market

A personification of the market created by Benjamin Graham. Mr. Market's often irrational and extreme mood swings allow the rational, patient investor opportune times to buy and sell investments.

Munger, Charlie

Chairman of Wesco Financial and partner of Warren Buffett at Wesco's parent company, Berkshire Hathaway. Munger is known for his terse satirical humor and, save for Buffett, is arguably the most intelligent investor of all time.

Mutual Fund

A financial instrument consisting of a basket of securities, usually stocks and bonds. A mutual fund typically includes a particular type of stock such as growth, large cap, small cap, value, and international to name a few. The main advantage of a mutual fund is investment diversification without excessive time and effort.

N

Narrow Moat

A rating used by Morningstar to describe a company that has a competitive advantage, but one that is relatively weak. Likewise, it can be used to describe a strong advantage that is not expected to last.

Nasdaq Composite Index

A stock index made of more than 3,000 companies traded on the technology-company-heavy Nasdaq stock exchange. "Nasdaq" is short for National Association of Securities Dealers Automated Quotations system.

Net Asset Value (NAV)

The value of a company derived by taking the total market value (not the book value) of its assets minus total liabilities.

Net Income

A company's total profit for a given time period, calculated as total revenues minus total expenses. This number may also be called "net profits," "the bottom line," or "net earnings."

Net Margin

Net income divided by total sales. Net margin (also known as net profit margin) is the percentage of every dollar in sales that translates to net income after all expenses have been subtracted. The higher this number, the more profitable the company.

Network Effect

A favorable competitive situation in which a company attracts additional customers by virtue of its existing customers. For example, as online auction firm eBay attracts more sellers, more buyers arrive, who in turn attract more sellers. It is an extremely desirable cycle, and one source of an economic moat.

New York Stock Exchange (NYSE)

One of the oldest and largest stock exchanges in the world. On an average day, more than 1 billion shares will be bought or sold on the exchange, which traces its origin back to 1792.

Nominating Committee

A part of a company typically responsible for nominating potential board members for election by shareholders.

Non-Interest-Bearing Liabilities

A liability that bears no interest rate. Non-interest-bearing liabilities typically appear due to accrual accounting. Examples include deferred revenue and accounts payable.

NOPAT

Net operating profit after tax. NOPAT is used to view a company's profitability as if it were not burdened by the cost of debt. This is what is typically used in the cash flow to the firm method of discounted cash-flow analysis.

Nygren, Bill

Successful value investor at Oakmark and Oakmark Select mutual funds, which have consistently outperformed the market.

O

Oligopoly
A situation in which a few firms dominate a certain market.

Operating Cash Flow
How much cash a company generates from its operations. Operating cash flow, which can be found in the top third of the statement of cash flows, can vary significantly from net income due to accrual accounting.

Operating Leverage
See the first definition of Leverage.

Operating Profit
Revenues minus the costs necessary to run the core businesses, such as cost of goods sold (COGS); selling, general, and administrative (SG&A) costs; depreciation and amortization; and research and development expenses. Operating profit is sometimes called EBIT (earnings before interest and taxes). It is a good indicator of the strength or weakness in the continuing operations of a company.

Oracle of Omaha
A common nickname for Warren Buffett.

Ordinary Income
An individual's income, such as wages and interest, that is taxed at ordinary income rates, as opposed to capital gains and dividends, which are taxed at their own rates.

Out of the Money
A term used to reference options whose strike price is below the current market price for puts and above the current market price for calls. Out-of-the-money options do not have intrinsic value.

Overconfidence
A behavioral finance term used to describe our tendency to think we are smarter, more talented, or more capable than we actually are.

P

Payout Ratio
The percentage of earnings that is paid to shareholders in the form of dividends.

PEG Ratio
An extension of the price/earnings ratio that accounts for earnings growth, calculated by dividing the forward P/E ratio by expected annual earnings per share (EPS) growth.

Pension Plan
A type of retirement plan set up by corporations that guarantees benefits for employees. In this scenario, the corporation bears the market risk,

whereas in a 401(k) retirement plan, benefits are based on employee contributions, and employees bear the market risk. 401(k) plans are quickly becoming the standard as pension plans are inherently inflexible and enormous costs can result.

Perpetuity Value

In a discounted cash-flow stock valuation, the value of a company beyond an explicit forecast period and into infinity.

Present Value

Today's value of future cash flows after being discounted by an appropriate discount rate. In a discounted cash-flow model, expected cash flows are discounted and then summed to find a company's current value. The opposite of this is future value—the present value is compounded (instead of discounted) for a certain number of periods at a particular rate to find an investment's worth in the future.

Present Value of Perpetuity

The value of a future perpetuity, discounted back to today's value. Calculating the present value of perpetuity is one of the final steps in performing a discounted cash-flow analysis.

Price/Book Ratio (P/B)

The market price of a company's outstanding stock divided by the company's book value. Book value is the total assets of a company less total liabilities, preferred stock, and intangible assets.

Price/Cash Flow

A stock's current price divided by the trailing 12-month operating cash flow per share. This is an indicator of a company's financial health.

Price/Earnings Ratio (P/E)

A stock's price divided by the stock's earnings per share. This is the most commonly referred to stock valuation metric.

Price/Sales Ratio (P/S)

A company's market capitalization divided by sales. The price/sales ratio represents the amount an investor is willing to pay for each dollar generated by a company's operations. This measure can be useful when the company in question has negative earnings or cash flow.

Principal

The par value of a bond that is paid to the lender (purchaser of the bond) upon maturity. In the case of a loan, such as a home mortgage, principal is the original amount loaned that is gradually amortized by the portion of each payment that is not interest.

Profit

Money generated in excess of money spent. This is why firms are in business. Gross profit and operating profit are common examples of profit measurements.

Prospectus

A legal document filed with the SEC (usually associated with an IPO) that outlines the purpose of the company, major risk factors, and planned use of the capital raised by the offering.

Proxy

An authorization through which a shareholder designates someone else (usually company management) to cast his or her vote in important company matters. The number of votes allowed per share of stock or whether any such votes exist will vary by company.

Proxy Fight

A dispute over a company matter that is taken to shareholders to decide. Proxy fights commonly occur in potential company takeover situations.

Proxy Statement

A statutory form required by the SEC that discloses various types of company information such as executive compensation, board of director nominations, and other issues that may or may not require a shareholder vote. Proxy statements are useful in gauging the long-term intentions of management. For example, will incentives given to management create intrinsic value for shareholders?

Public Filings

The various reports and documents required by law to be made available to investors. Common examples are 10-Qs and 10-Ks, which are collected and reviewed by the Securities and Exchange Commission (SEC).

Publicly Traded

A company is publicly traded when a portion of its shares is available for sale and purchase on a stock exchange. A firm becomes publicly traded through an IPO with the usual purpose of raising capital for a company.

Put

An option represented by a contract that allows the purchaser to sell a stock to a second party within a certain amount of time. The other party, or "writer of the put," is obligated to buy the stock, and is compensated for this risk by a premium—the price of the contract. The put holder will exercise the option only when the strike price of the put is more than the current market price. The difference between these two numbers less the premium paid is the put holder's gain.

Q

Qualified Dividend

Dividends from most domestic corporations and some foreign corporations that are eligible for the 15% dividend tax rate. Requirements include a minimum holding period and that the position was unhedged.

Quarterly Report
See 10-Q.

R

Rate of Return
The return of an investment divided by the original amount invested, usually stated in an annualized amount.

Ratio-Based Approach
The use of common financial ratios, such as P/E and P/B, to value stocks.

Real Estate Investment Trust (REIT)
Pooled investor funds used for investment in many types of real estate. REITs trade on an exchange like stocks, which makes them more liquid than direct real estate investment. Due to their favorable tax treatment, they are required to pay dividends regardless of share appreciation.

Real Return
The rate of return adjusted for inflation, calculated as the nominal (actual) rate minus the inflation rate. For example, if inflation last year was 3% and a return of 10% was realized on an investment, the real rate of return was only 7%.

Regret
In the context of behavioral finance, the disappointment or distress that influences our ability to distinguish a bad decision from a bad outcome.

Representativeness
A mental shortcut that causes us to give too much weight to recent evidence—such as short-term performance numbers—and too little weight to the evidence from the more distant past.

Required Rate of Return
The return required by investors to compensate for the risk they assume when purchasing debt or stock.

Restructuring Charges
Expenses that a company realizes as the result of a structural change caused by a shift in strategy, a merger or acquisition, or asset devaluation. Investors should be leery of companies that repeatedly use these supposedly "one-time" charges to hide larger operating issues.

Return on Assets (ROA)
A measure of a company's efficiency and profitability. Boiled down, it is calculated as net income divided by total assets. There is no rule as to what is a good ROA, so it is best to analyze this measure within the context of a firm's particular industry. ROA is usually stated as a percentage.

Return on Capital (ROC)
See Return on Invested Capital.

Return on Equity (ROE)
An efficiency measure calculated as net income from the income statement divided by shareholders' equity on the

balance sheet. ROE can also be calculated as ROA times a company's financial leverage. The purpose of this measure is to see how much profit the company is producing with money invested by shareholders. ROE is usually stated as a percentage.

Return on Invested Capital (ROIC)

Arguably the most important profitability measure, calculated as NOPAT divided by total assets, minus excess cash and non-interest-bearing liabilities. This is a good indication of how effectively a company allocates and uses its capital. ROIC is usually stated as a percentage.

Return on Stock

See Total Shareholder Return.

Revenue

A line item from the income statement that represents the dollar amount of goods and services sold by a company. Note that this does not necessarily represent the cash a company received because some sales are made on credit, which would increase the receivables account.

Revenue Recognition

The process by which revenue is earned and recorded by a company. Due to accrual accounting, when a company recognizes revenue can vary significantly from when a company collects the cash from selling its goods or services.

Risk-Free Rate

Typically refers to the rate of return on United States Treasury securities. Although theoretically possible, the U.S. government would have to go bankrupt for these bills, notes, and bonds to default. So far, this has never occurred.

Risk Premium

The additional return required by investors for taking on additional risk. The risk premium can be related to a variety of investments: the premium required on stocks versus bonds, the premium required for a particular stock over the general market (as in CAPM), or the premium of an investment over the risk-free rate.

Roth IRA

A type of individual retirement account (IRA) that allows for tax-free accumulation of savings. Investors who qualify can contribute aftertax dollars to Roth IRAS, and withdrawals are tax-free, subject to certain rules.

Royalty Trust

An investment vehicle that derives its income from royalties, typically on the production of natural resources. Royalty trusts can have very high yields, but those yields can vary significantly over time.

Ruane, Bill

A value investor taught by Benjamin Graham in the same classroom as Warren Buffett. Ruane is founder and chairman of Sequoia Fund, which has consistently beaten the S&P 500 Index.

Rule of 72

A shorthand method of estimating the number of years it will take for an investment to double in value at a given interest rate. It is calculated as 72/(interest rate). For example, an investment receiving 10% interest per year would approximately double in 7.2 years (72/10).

S

S&P 500 Index

A stock index composed of 500 large U.S. companies chosen based on market size, liquidity, and group representation. Like the Dow, the S&P 500 is often used to gauge the health of the overall stock market and as a benchmark for the performance of investment portfolios.

Securities and Exchange Commission (SEC)

The federal regulatory agency with the responsibility of protecting investors by ensuring fair transactions and adequate disclosure of relevant information in the financial markets.

Selective Memory

Remembering an event or action in a way that may be more favorable, and less accurate or objective, particularly if the event or action was painful. Selective memory can be a detrimental behavior when investing.

Self-Handicapping

Explaining any possible poor performance with a reason that may or may not be true.

Selling, General, and Administrative Expenses (SG&A)

Expenses found on the income statement that result from various corporate activities not directly associated with a product's cost, such as utility bills, payroll, advertising, leases for corporate headquarters, and others.

Share Buybacks

The purchase of a company's shares by the company itself. Buybacks are generally considered a shareholder-friendly action taken by management when it feels the price of company stock is below its intrinsic value. Buybacks lower the outstanding share count, increasing earnings per share, and thereby increasing the value of shares held by shareholders.

Shareholders

The owners of the stock of a company. Management should always strive to benefit shareholders by increasing the intrinsic value of their firms through the profitable allocation of resources. Shareholders have the responsibility to voice their opinion of management's actions by voting their proxies.

Shareholders' Equity

The estimated accounting value of a company. It is generally calculated as assets minus liabilities. In other words, equity is the difference between the value of what a company owns and what it owes.

Shares

The denomination of ownership in a company. The more shares you own of a company, the greater your ownership stake. Shares, or stocks, used to be represented by paper certificates, but these have been largely replaced with electronic accounts.

Shorting

A speculative venture that results in a gain when the price of a stock falls instead of rises. The stock is borrowed and immediately sold at current market prices. If the stock price drops as expected, the stock is repurchased at the new lower price and returned to the lender. Think of it as trying to sell high and buy low, in that order. Shorting is a risky way to make money since potential losses are unlimited, while gains are capped at the original sale price.

Special Dividend

A one-time dividend that is substantially larger than a normal dividend, usually reflecting an exceptionally strong earnings period, a desired change in the company's financial structure, or a company's inability to find adequate returns on a growing hoard of cash. Microsoft's $32 billion ($3 per share) special dividend in 2004 is a good example of the latter.

Spin-off

An independent company created from a portion of an existing company that is sold as a whole unit, or through a public offering of shares. A company may cleave a portion of itself in order to focus on other parts of the business, or to capitalize on the high prices being paid in the stock market for the portion of the business being sold.

Statement of Cash Flows

A financial statement showing how much cash has gone in and out of a company over a specific time period, such as three months or one year. The statement of cash flows, which is one of the three main financial statements, adjusts for certain transactions that may affect income but do not result in cash flows.

Stewardship

A measure of how well company executives are doing their jobs, and whose best interests they have in mind. Increasing shareholder value should always be the supreme concern.

Stock

See Shares.

Stock Dividend

The distribution of additional shares to current shareholders instead of cash dividends. This method of paying shareholders is uncommon today.

Stock Split

A process whereby a company issues new shares to existing stockholders. The most common stock split is 2-for-1, which means that an investor who owned one share before the stock split will own two shares afterward, each at half of the old value. A stock split does not change the overall value of a company; it just changes the number of shares.

Stop-Loss Order

An order placed with a broker that designates a particular sell price for a stock that is below the current market price. Stop-loss orders are designed to limit an investor's loss.

Street Lag

A term coined by Peter Lynch referencing all the buying activity that has likely preceded a buy recommendation by a broker. Unfortunately, many brokers will not recommend a particular stock to their clients until there has been sufficient institutional purchasing, which validates the stock's "investment worthiness" in the broker's mind. By this time, the stock is often overpriced, which is precisely when you shouldn't buy.

Strike Price

The price at which an option allows the purchaser to either sell or buy the underlying security, usually a stock. The holder of a call option profits when the stock price rises above the strike price, whereas the holder of a put option profits when the stock price falls below the strike price.

Sunk Cost Fallacy

A behavioral finance theory stating that we are unable to ignore the "sunk costs" of a decision, even when those costs are unlikely to be recovered.

Supplier Power

One of Michael Porter's Five Forces that references the ability of suppliers to demand profitable prices for their goods and services. Any firm that is at the mercy of its suppliers will have a hard time making ends meet.

Sustainable Growth

The growth in earnings a company could theoretically achieve assuming current profitability and the dividend payout rate are held constant, calculated as ROE x (1 – payout ratio). *See Payout Ratio and Return on Equity.*

Switching Costs

Inconveniences or expenses a customer incurs in order to switch from one product to another. Companies want their customers to have high switching costs because this widens companies' economic moats.

Systematic Risk

Market risk that is not diversifiable. Systematic risk affects the valuation of all stocks through macroeconomic variables such as recessions and changes in monetary policy (interest rates) and fiscal policy (tax structure).

T

Taxable Account

An investment account not sheltered from taxes. This means you have to pay taxes on any interest payments or dividends, as well as on any capital gains you realize when investments are sold. With tax-deferred accounts, such as IRAs and 401(k)s, you can postpone the payment of these taxes.

Tax-Deferred

An account, such as an IRA or 401(k), that lets you postpone paying taxes on your earnings. Because more of your money works for you through compounding, tax deferral allows you to earn more over time.

Tax Rate

The percentage of earnings paid in taxes, calculated by dividing earnings before taxes by taxes paid.

Threat of Substitutes

One of Michael Porter's Five Forces that references the possibility of competitors creating a product that can effectively replace another firm's products. Optimally a company tries to create a product or service that is not easily replaced by a rival's offering.

Time Value

The value of an option that is based on the length of time until expiration. Time is important when valuing an option. The option holder wants to have more time between now and the option's expiration date to allow for the possibility of price changes. Time combined with a volatile stock makes the chance of an option becoming in the money much more likely. As an option reaches its expiration date, the premium investors are willing to pay diminishes until it reaches zero on expiration day.

Total Return

The return of a stock based on its price appreciation as well as its dividends. A common measure of total return is called the holding period return and is calculated as current price minus purchase price (capital gains), plus dividends.

Transparency

The degree to which a company's financial and operational disclosures are clearly presented. Legal jargon and diversion tactics can severely limit the transparency of a company's financial statements. Generally, the more opaque the language in disclosures, the more the company has to hide. On the other hand, the Berkshire Hathaway annual report is a great example of transparent disclosure.

U

Unitholder
An investor who holds units in a master limited partnership. Unitholders are essentially the same as shareholders in a corporation. They receive distributions (similar to dividends) and can benefit from price appreciation of their units.

Unsystematic Risk
The unique risk inherent to a specific company or stock that can be offset through diversification (also known as diversifiable risk).

V

Valuation
The process of determining how much a company is worth. There are many ways to value a company. The method focused on in these workbooks is the discounted cash-flow (DCF) method.

Volatility
The degree of fluctuation in the price of a stock. High volatility indicates that the stock's price has experienced significant ups and downs in the past, whereas low volatility indicates that the stock's price has been relatively stable. A common measure of volatility is beta, which measures price change relative to a market index. A beta greater than one indicates that the stock is more volatile than the index, whereas a beta less than one indicates that the stock is less volatile than the index.

W

Wanger, Ralph
The successful investor who in 1992 founded Columbia Wanger Asset Management, which invests using value-oriented principles.

Weighted Average Cost of Capital (WACC)
The weighted average of the cost of debt and the cost of equity for a given company. When performing a cash flow to the firm method of discounted cash-flow analysis, all future cash flows are discounted by this percentage and then summed to determine present value. Higher WACCs indicate a greater uncertainty surrounding future cash flows, which appropriately results in lower valuations of those future cash flows.

Whisper Stock
A stock that is getting a lot of subtle attention as a potential breakout performer. Tips received through a whisper, or any other method for that matter, should be taken with skepticism and carefully analyzed on a fundamental basis before considering investment.

Whitman, Marty

The chairman of Third Avenue Funds who has achieved great success through value investing.

Woodstock for Capitalists

Common name for the Berkshire Hathaway annual shareholder meeting, as well as the name of a documentary profiling this event. It attracts thousands of attendees every year, and is chaired by Warren Buffett and Charlie Munger.

Writer

The seller of an option contract. The writer has the obligation to provide the underlying stock, in the case of a call, and to buy the underlying stock, in the case of a put, from the buyer of the written contract. Writing options is risky because of the large loss potential with the upside limited to the premium—the price of the contract.

Y

Yield

See Dividend Yield.

Formulas Reference

Valuation Ratios

Market Capitalization = Stock Price × Shares Outstanding

Enterprise Value = Market Capitalization + Debt − Cash

P/E = Stock Price ÷ EPS = Market Capitalization ÷ Total Company Profits

Earnings Yield = 1 ÷ P/E = EPS ÷ Stock Price

PEG = Forward P/E ÷ 5-Year EPS Growth Rate

P/S = Stock Price ÷ Sales Per Share = Market Capitalization ÷ Total Sales

P/B = Stock Price ÷ Book Value Per Share =
Market Capitalization ÷ Total Shareholder Equity

Book Value Per Share = Total Shareholder Equity ÷ Shares Outstanding

P/CF = Stock Price ÷ Operating Cash Flow Per Share =
Market Capitalization ÷ Total Operating Cash Flow

Accounting

Assets = Liabilities + Equity

Gross Profit = Net Revenue − Cost of Sales

Operating Income = Gross profit − SG&A − Depreciation − Amortization −
Other Operating Expenses − Restructuring Expenses

Net Income = Operating Income − Tax Expense − Interest Expense −
Any Other Nonoperating Expense

continued…

continued...

Basic EPS = Net income ÷ No. of Basic Wtd. Avg. Shares Outstanding

Diluted EPS = Net Income / No. of Diluted Wtd. Avg. Shares Outstanding

Free Cash Flow = Operating Cash Flow – Capital Expenditures

Company Efficiency and Financial Health Metrics

Inventory Turnover = Cost of Sales ÷ Average Inventory

Accounts Receivable Turnover = Revenue ÷ Average Accounts Receivable

Accounts Payable Turnover = Cost of Sales ÷ Average Accounts Payable

Total Asset Turnover = Revenue ÷ Average Total Assets

Current Ratio = Current Assets ÷ Current Liabilities

Quick Ratio = (Cash + Accounts Receivable + Short-Term or Marketable Investments) ÷ Current Liabilities

Cash Ratio = (Cash + Short-Term or Marketable Investments) ÷ Current Liabilities

Debt/Equity = (Short-Term Debt + Long-Term Debt) ÷ Total Equity

Interest Coverage = Operating Income ÷ Interest Expense

Gross Margin = Gross Profit (or Loss) ÷ Sales

Operating Margin = Operating Income (or Loss) ÷ Sales

Net Margin = Net Income (or Loss) ÷ Sales

Free Cash Flow Margin = Free Cash Flow ÷ Sales

ROA "traditional" = (Net Income + Aftertax Interest Expense) ÷ Average Total Assets

Aftertax Interest Expense = $(1 - \text{Tax Rate}) \times$ Interest Expense

ROA "DuPont" = Asset Turnover × Net Profit Margin

ROE "traditional" = Net Income ÷ Average Shareholders' Equity

ROE "DuPont" = Asset Turnover × Net Profit Margin × Asset/Equity Ratio

ROIC = Net Operating Profit, After Taxes (NOPAT) ÷ Invested Capital (IC)

Net Operating Profit, After Taxes (NOPAT) = Operating Profit × $(1 - \text{Tax Rate})$

Invested Capital (IC) = Total Assets − Excess Cash − Non-Interest-Bearing Current Liabilities

Cash Return = (Free Cash Flow + Net Interest Expense) ÷ Enterprise Value

Time Value of Money and DCF

Approximate Time Required for Money to Double = 72 ÷ Annual Rate of Return

Future Value = Present Value $\times (1 + i)^N$

i = Interest (your rate of return or interest rate earned)
N = Number of Years (the length of time you invest)

Present Value of CF in Year N = CF at Year $N \div (1 + R)^N$

CF = Cash Flow
R = Required Return (Discount Rate)
N = Number of Years in the Future

continued...

continued...

Perpetuity Value $= \text{CFn} \times (1 + g) \div (R - g)$

CFn = Cash Flow in the Last Individual Year Estimated
g = Long-Term Growth Rate
R = Discount Rate, or Cost of Capital

Weighted Average Cost of Capital (WACC) = (Weight of Debt)(Cost of Debt) + (Weight of Equity)(Cost of Equity)

Graham's Intrinsic Value Formulas

Value = Current (Normal) Earnings ×
(8.5 + Twice the Expected Annual Growth Rate)

Approximate P/E = (8.5 + Twice the Expected Annual Growth Rate)

Expected Growth = (Stock Price − 8.5) ÷ (2 × Current Earnings)

Dividends and Sustainable Growth

Dividend Yield = Annual Dividends Per Share ÷ Current Stock Price

Payout Ratio = Dividends Per Share ÷ EPS

Required Retention Ratio (R3) = Expected Growth Rate ÷ ROE

Sustainable Growth = ROE × (1 − Payout Ratio)

Cost of Growth = R3 × Normalized EPS

Excess Earnings Yield = (Normalized EPS − Dividends Per Share − Cost of Growth) ÷ Current Share Price

Total Expected Return = Dividend Yield + Expected Profit Growth + Excess Earnings Yield

More Stock Workbooks in the Morningstar Investing Series

How to Get Started in Stocks
Get up to speed on the basics, including why you should consider stock investing and how to think like an analyst.

How to Select Winning Stocks
Learn how to interpret financial statements, place a value on business, and find financially strong companies for potential investment.

Also Learn the Ins and Outs of Successful Fund Investing with Morningstar Mutual Funds Workbooks

Find the Right Mutual Funds
For beginners searching for funds that will best meet their investing objectives.

Diversify Your Fund Portfolio
For investors with a little experience who want to improve their skills, techniques, and portfolios.

Maximize Your Fund Returns
For experienced fund investors looking for new ways to improve the value of their portfolios.

10 Free Morningstar Stock Analyst Reports

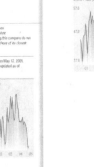